thou shalt give birth to a comma happy, savage good life

JENNIFER ELLIOTT

*thou shalt give birth to a
comma happy, savage
good life*

dedication

This book is dedicated to my firstborn, Tanner, who had to endure more than any other child while I got my shit together. He is one of the reasons I am where I am today. Without my need to give him a good life, who knows where I would be? So, on October 2nd, 2004, I began a journey of finding self-contentment so that I could have a comma happy, savage good life to raise him in.

And oh—what a ride it has been!

contents

BIRTH CANAL—PASSAGEWAY TO LIFE

MY REBIRTH

There was a time in my life when I went through the motions. I felt suffocated. I couldn't catch my breath; I couldn't catch a break. I lived day-to-day, and frankly, life was hard and unenjoyable. I was living paycheck to paycheck...drowning and hitting dead ends quite frequently.

I made change after change and somehow kept falling into low, low times. At one point in my life, I hit rock bottom—I just knew then that it was the end. I was as low as I could get, and I had no answers to get myself back out of that pit.

I recognize now that it was never just a hard fall. It was a slow descent with some spikes upward in between. You see, I went through periods of trauma and pain early on in life, then I fell into some addictive habits, and I hit hard times where I literally only had myself to rely on...

It was during these times of self-reliance that I learned about myself. I navigated my mind, my body, my wants, my needs—my mental, emotional, physical, and spiritual obligations to myself...I delved deep into who I am, why I settled, how I gravitated towards certain things, and why I went through the things I did.

To get through these times, I first sat down and wrote a list of things that made me happy. I realized what made me happy was making other people happy, so then I sat down and wrote a list of random acts of kindness and made it a point to try to do something from both lists as often as possible. Daily if I could.

I also understood that when I was going through anguish, I couldn't let it sit inside and fester. I had to release it somehow. It had to find its way out of my being and into something else. Yes, these times in my life happened, but they do not make up my entire story and they cannot occupy me any longer. So I let it go and let it live somewhere else. It lived in my poetry. It lived in music. It lived in my need to make the world a better place.

I thought about not only my goals and passions but how I could use them to fulfill my purpose, help myself and help those around me. I've learned that bad shit happens and I have accepted that when ugly goes on around me, it is out of my hands to prevent it.

Instead of paralyzing myself into numbness over something I couldn't control, I started focusing on what good could come out of bad situations. I started looking for the good people out there doing the hard work not to help correct it, but to ease the pain and mold it into a different direction, altering each step I took, ultimately altering my entire journey. Even when the world around me seemed to be crumbling, I learned to fixate on that which is good and turned my heart away from the ugly unless it was to help people through it.

I have learned to accept the journey I am on, hold compassion for all, but still discern the difference between good and bad —and put on my armor of protection when my spidey senses are tingling.

After all, bad things do not define us. And once we can put ourselves first, work on filling our cups daily, donning our own oxygen masks before we help others, and prioritizing self-care, then we can be fully available to care for and help those around us.

I work hard every single day to maintain my happiness and contentment within myself. Sometimes, that means having to start over again and again, and that's okay. I've accepted that, too. That's also a part of self-care. Taking charge of my happiness was hard for me. It was so easy for me to blame other people for my hard times. But at the end of the day, I have the ability within myself to alter my mindset, change my perspective, and reroute when needed.

Perhaps this won't make sense until you have read my story and walked my journey, and I am excited that you have picked this book up to take this first step with me. The term "comma happy" has stuck with me for quite some time now. I first heard the term while providing content writing for a company I worked for years ago, and I was told that I was too comma happy—pretty much noting that I use wayyyy too many commas. I took this as a compliment. You see, I have always been one to enjoy a good pause. A pause between two parts of a sentence, a pause in life.

Same thing.

As you go through this book, take notice of all the times I have paused and waited on what to do next. Sometimes, my pauses were a good cry or a breath of fresh air. Sometimes, my pauses were an entire hiatus or time away from my "real" life. But in the end, I always found myself again and took a moment to reflect on the purpose of me going through an event so I could see the bigger picture of where it fell in my life. My life commas are my biggest form of self-love I can give.

"Ubuntu" has been a term that I hold dear. It is an African

concept that means "humanity to others," and in a way, it also means "other's humanity to me." It has shaped my mentality into the idea that I am me because of all the people I encounter throughout my life. Even though I consider myself to be somewhat antisocial, I feel deeply for others. So the idea that I am molded and shaped by those with whom I come in contact throughout my life hits me hard. I am selective with who I allow in, and for good reason. But the very concept of self-love and love for others has defined me and given me a SAVAGE good life that I want to share with others.

When I think of the word savage, I think of being fierce, bold, brave and unafraid. A warrior even. A savage is someone who doesn't care about the opinions of others and will do what they need to do for themselves, even if it makes others wonder if they are crazy. A term that comes to mind is BAD-ASS! And to have a savage good life is to have the balls to do what others may not do in order to live a life that many cannot live. A person who is savage is real, raw, and able to find radical happiness because they don't rely on anyone else to find it and they don't give a fuck what other people think.

I don't always have all the answers. I wouldn't ever say life is easy, but right now at this point in my life, I am content. I find peace, love, and happiness within myself. I do not find it within anyone else. Even though it may sometimes come from others, no one else has that kind of power over me because I hold the power of my well-being all within myself.

And you have that power within you, too! It was in you all along. We just have to dig deep and find it. Sometimes we let life take over. We say we will do it when the time is right or when life gets easier. But there is never a better time than now to take charge of your contentment...even if it feels a little too hard to do. And even if we have to do so in more manageable segments.

Many times, I have had to put extensive work into my self-happiness. I've had my share of trials and troubles, and at times, life demanded more than I had to give. I've had many moments where my self-worth was tested, and I may have even given up on myself a time or two, each time starting over with a new pause, a new beginning, a new outlook, and a new path.

I have learned that my life is made up of many little stepping stones and people weaving in and out of my life that lead to the next big thing, followed by more tiny stepping stones and more people (and some people leaving) that all make up this crazy journey I am on. When I break it down into steps instead of the entire trip, it becomes manageable and even enjoyable, even during some not-so-good moments. Those little pauses I purposely take for myself, and even the ones forced on me, really help me refresh and reset.

I'm not even sure where these pauses throughout my life come from! Some call it God, some divine intervention, some just feel a tug like the Universe is giving a good push to assist and provide answers. I've become fully committed to digging deep inside myself by allowing my spirit to guide me. I've taken my needed pauses for self-reflection, and in doing so, I have mastered the art of true self-contentment—and you can too!

This book was written initially for myself to preserve my memories. But as I started writing, I realized others may understand some pieces of my journey, relate to it, and even get a lift from some of the internal searching I governed over myself. Your journey is different from mine, but perhaps we can work together to find goodness all around us even during bad times.

This book is designed to be interactive. At the end of each chapter, I have composed some thoughtful questions to encourage you to self-reflect on where you are and where you want to be. Take your time and really dig inside yourself. Come out of your shell and come alive with your pen in hand. Pour your heart onto these pages in self-reflection. Remember, life is about each step we take. Step by step, we have the power to take control of our journey. We can't always regulate perfection or sway from all harm and ruin, but we can fortify ourselves from within, and we can do so quickly, even before we make it to that next stepping stone.

We are high-caliber beings, worthy of bountiful blessings. And the secret is—we must entrust this fragile care only to ourselves without relying on anyone else to fulfill our own needs of worth, love, peace, and happiness. Invest in yourself. Learn yourself. Hold high regard for yourself. Take time to smell the roses on your road to self-contentment and really find pleasure in just being you. Just BE, and be FREE inside of yourself—a roamer of sorts, a nomad, always wandering to find greener pastures at all times. We don't ever have to stay in bad situations and can quickly reroute.

I am the queen of side trips in my journeys. After all, there isn't a map to follow. If you go too far forward, you can always go back. If you aren't where you want to be, you can always go on a different path. If you like where you are, you can pause as long as you need to until something else shifts and you have to adjust. ***Comma Happy* means when you love where you are at, you stay there as long as you can.** Enjoy those pauses given to you at just the right time in your life...

Comma Happy

"You're too Comma Happy," she said.
"You take too many breaks between words."
"You take too many pauses, Jennifer..."
She said, "Not every pause warrants a comma,"
But I beg to differ.

I'm the queen of a good pause.
Timeouts. Side trips. Intermissions. Recess.
A good 9th inning stretch. An admirable halftime show.
A breath of fresh air off the patio.
A catnap when needed. A coffee break.
A halt, and sometimes, even an about-face
In the opposite direction.
A much-needed vacation.
A leisurely stroll. A tear shed. A life of ease.
Even in the shambles, I manage to breathe.
A lingering memory. Lost in my thoughts.
Take time for myself. Rest when needed.
In the midst of chaos.
I'm calm and relaxed. Happy in fact.
A dilly, a dally.
A road trip to who cares where.
A wink. An embrace. Smell the flowers.
A departure to somewhere far away.
Happy hour.
A song. A movie. Take time for a game.
A move across the country, if that's what it takes.
A little trip to secret places, even if it happens just in my mind.
Just to get away.
A dip in the ocean.
A private thought. A puppy snuggle. A dream.
My survival depends on these little things.
From a tiny hiatus to big retreats.
I've gotten this far due to these moments.
These pauses in time.
Comma happy.
Peace in the instant's contentment is needed most.
Stay in these spaces as long as you need to.

Adjust when you must.
Enjoy the pauses given to you
At just the right time in your life.
Enjoy the ride.
The road you are on.
Wherever it takes you.
Do it for you.
You can ride out anything thrown at you.
Live life. A vagabond. A nomad. Carefree.
A SAVAGE good life when you master COMMA HAPPY.

Part of Comma Happy is also getting to this place of contentment, and then helping those around you, the people you love and care for, reach this same level of complacency and fulfillment.

According to Maslow's hierarchy of needs, there are levels that range from very basic needs to high-rise needs. If the needs at the bottom of the pyramid aren't met, you can't possibly meet those needs at the top. Because of this, you have to master the basics in order to master your higher self. This pyramid begins with the physiological needs of things like food, sleep, shelter, air, drink, etc. Next, we must acknowledge your safety needs. Safety is very important to your wellness. Physical safety, healthcare access, financial safety, and more. After this, you can head to social belonging. This includes love, friendships, family, and emotional intimacy. This can mean something different to everyone, but who wants to be alone and unloved? The next stepping stone is esteem. This is the esteem of others and the esteem of self. You want others to hold you in high regard, but we also must hold ourselves high.

In Maslow's hierarchy of needs, we look at your cognitive and aesthetic needs...the need for knowledge, the need to explore, the need to learn. The need to experience beauty and wander. And finally, you go all the way up to self-actualization. Fulfilling your own potential. Knowing yourself and being satisfied with where you are in life.

And the other part of that top tier is self-transcendence. Altruistically helping others meet their needs. Getting to the top and then pulling those around you up to the top with you. In fact, Maslow added to this theory throughout his life and even wrote, "Transcendence refers to the very highest and most inclusive or holistic levels of human consciousness, behaving and relating, as ends rather than means, to oneself, to significant others, to human beings in general, to other species, to nature, and to the cosmos." Spirituality perhaps?

Either way, we have the power within us to meet not only our basic needs but also these high-caliber inner needs. Remember, you are the captain of your ship...pilot of your plane and driver of your car. Well, you get what I am saying. Because you are in charge of your journey!

Aaannnnddd with that—let's dive right in!

my birthing story

chapter 1

THOU SHALT NOT LET TRAUMA DEFINE YOU

Before I share my secrets to contentment, I first must share with you the bumpy road I traveled to get here. While I will not dwell on where I have been, I do feel it is worthy to make note of some of the struggles I have had to face to get to where I am right now. Many times, I thought my journey would break me, but it has actually made me stronger.

I had a great childhood in my early years. My father worked, and my mother stayed home with my brother and me. Those were my favorite times. She crocheted a lot, and having learned to crochet with her around age six or so, we spent a lot of time making blankets and other items together.

As I recall it, at one point, my father didn't work much. My mother stepped up and worked a couple of jobs to make sure we had what we needed. We didn't have a lot, but we were not in need. I remember little tidbits—like the one time we did have a car, it didn't have doors and was pretty unsafe to ride in. But most of my childhood was spent taking the city bus, which was fine by me. We didn't know any better, so we didn't want anything else. It was our normal, and I was content.

I have photos of me at different amusement parks, petting zoos, swimming pools, etc., so I reckon we did a lot of things together as a family. Some photos had my father in them. A lot of photos had my grandparents with us. We had some pretty good times. I don't remember much (a common theme throughout my life), but around age eight, my life took a turn, and I was shattered...my father left, and that very act determined most of my life thoughts, choices, and decisions.

Once my father left, my mother had to work even more in order to provide. Yes, she was used to working a lot, even while my dad was around, but she had more pressure and more at stake without his help. Before he left, he would take us to see her at work. Now, she would have less time with us. She worked very hard to pay the bills, make sure we were fed, and make sure we had a roof over our heads.

In fact, during this time that my mother navigated single parenthood, I began watching her. I conceived this fight inside myself. I birthed this need to survive, this fierce work ethic, and this raging determination to be somebody and to find contentment and success, whatever that meant to me at the time. I cultivated and babied this strength that I was acquiring from experiencing and watching the actions my mother demonstrated in sheer desperation.

Being a fatherless child defined my entire being for a great portion of my childhood. It affected the quality of my life and altered my reality throughout my entire adolescence. I spent a lot of time angry as hell and hurt beyond belief. I went through all the phases of grieving, which according to the Kubler-Ross model, consists of denial, anger, bargaining, depression, and acceptance. I knew my father was still alive, so it wasn't that type of grief, but I still went through mourning nonetheless. As I found out twenty years later, he was, indeed, alive; he just lived a life in New York City my entire adolescence. He was making another family for himself there.

But during this time of being a newly fatherless child, I spent some time in shock. I isolated myself, became angry, and suffered through depression, whatever depression looks like for an eight-year-old. Sometimes, I went back and forth between all of these feelings. I remember wandering the streets of my small town, just looking everywhere, trying to find my father. When I wasn't trying to find him, I was at home writing or listening to solemn music. I found a love for classical music during this time.

When my father first left, I didn't partake in any harmful methods of dealing with this new life, probably because I was young and innocent. That would come later. I was pretty sheltered for a long time...I do remember focusing a lot on school. I didn't really have many friends. That's also a common theme throughout my life. Maybe I was afraid to get too close to anyone for fear of them leaving, too. But I did spend a lot of time working on school work, getting homework turned in, doing all the extra credit, being a part of the National Honor Society, and doing anything I could do to please my teachers. I had perfect attendance throughout all of my school years. It was an accomplishment and something I could control.

I also stayed busy with as many activities as I could. I was in indoor guard, outdoor colorguard, chorus, and orchestra. I went to church programs, Friday Night Fire (a musical program with a different church), Sunday programs, and camping trips through the church—whatever I could get into to keep my mind occupied. I still stay quite busy well into my adulthood.

Throughout all of this, I eventually accepted that this was my life. I accepted it...but I still had to work my way through figuring out how I would explore this new life. As a child being raised by a single parent, I also had to almost raise my brother and myself because my mother spent so much time earning a living to provide for us.

I learned that poetry was a good escape for me, and it has been my main way of coping or getting through hard times. It allows me to pour my heart out onto the paper, and it releases me from whatever I am feeling. It has also helped me finalize times in my life so I can start over. It refreshes my thoughts. By orchestrating the scenarios of my mind, I have found pardon within myself...relief from what I was feeling...a clear mind to then feel free to go on to my next stepping stone. My way of starting over is to just take a step in a different direction.

I have started over more than once, and I am sure my days of new beginnings are not over yet. One of my very first poetic arrangements concerned my father and revolved around the very act of him leaving. At such a young age I sure felt deep...I penned this somewhere around age nine.

Daddy, Come Home
Where are you, Daddy? You're supposed to be here.
I cannot find you!! You aren't anywhere near.

These memories are killing me...
Things aren't as they used to be.
I thought you loved me...

I'm waiting patiently,
I need to tell you about these feelings
going on inside of me.

I find myself screaming.
I cry myself to sleep at night.
I keep wishing you would hear me.

You've caused all this misery
Bound, chained inside of me.
You're not here where you should be.
You deprived me of a family.

How could you just walk away?
We are not safe
I'm struggling even facing each day.
If only you could hear me pray,
While quiet tears roll down my face.
My future isn't even clear.
I need you here.

I lie awake at night, asking myself
What I did to cause you to leave.
This is where you should be,
I deserve to be happy,
But you left, and you're not even sorry.
You changed my future forever.

By the time I entered middle school, I had spent so much time reflecting. I don't recall ever acting out my anger on anyone else because I recognized that my father caused this void in my life. It was my father's choice to leave. And to be honest, for a long time I was very embarrassed to be the child without the father. So, for quite a while, I felt if I didn't talk about it, it didn't happen...until I had to acknowledge that it did happen. And he wasn't here. And I had no one to enjoy father/daughter dances with. And family time sucked. Like, really sucked.

Well into my middle school years, I wasn't in complete acceptance yet. However, I was definitely working towards that goal. I began to realize that accepting my circumstances aided me in my recovery. I began to recognize that maybe my father leaving was a part of the big plan in store for my life. This acceptance inside of me wasn't for anyone else but solely for my inner peace. After a lot of reflection and working through some inner turmoil, I got to this place where I could at least begin to think about working through my affliction. I maybe even started finding some appreciation for where I was at in life.

BLESSED

How could you leave, not saying goodbye?
Making me cry
Leaving me all alone, wondering why!
I am somewhat depressed.

I should have begged you to stay
Would you have still gone away?
But I realize today,
That it was for the best.

My life would not have been the same
For my tomorrow or today
If you had decided to stay
I should consider myself blessed.

I took a lot of pauses during this time. At that moment of my life, this looked more like explorations of myself. I walked around my neighborhood a lot. I spent time in the cemetery, walking the train tracks, finding secret trails to venture. These places allowed me to have complete solitude. I rarely ran into a human in any of these locations. I enjoyed time alone.

My pauses were time with nature and time with myself. I began exploring spirituality. Feeling one with the earth. I got lost a lot. Sometimes, I felt like I had to lose myself to find myself. I had to lose thoughts and perceptions in order to find truth and reality.

I remember blaming myself a lot. I thought, *If only I listened better or did what I was told. If I helped more around the house or hugged more. If I showed love more, maybe he would have stayed.* I've never been an affectionate person, even as a child, so of course these thoughts lingered in the back of my mind often in everything I did.

I internalized these thoughts of self-accusation way more than I should have. It made sense at the time and took me a long time, even into adulthood, to realize that there really wasn't anything I could have done or not done to change the situation. Still, the very act of my father leaving was ingrained in me so deep. I let it define me for a lot of my life.

To paint a better picture of who I was—I was an ugly child. I had huge teeth, huge glasses, wild, frizzy hair from the perms my mother used to give me, and my mother crocheted a lot of my clothes. I never really fit in, and maybe I didn't care to fit in. I had a few amazing friends more into my high school years who accepted me for who I was, and I still talk to them today. My circle was small then, and I still live that way. Aside from being picked on for the way I looked and dressed a lot of my life, I had a decent childhood. I don't have very many bad memories.

There was this one December day, around the time that my father left, when we headed off to church. There, my mother sang a solo: "O' Holy Night." It's funny how certain things leave your memory, but other things stick in your head forever so vividly like it happened just yesterday. I still cry when I hear that song. When we were done at church that day, we walked back home. I remember so lucidly that the door we left from was chained shut, so we went to the other door and it was wide open...thieves had taken everything! They even took all of our Christmas gifts! It's not like we had a lot to begin with, so that was a particularly hard Christmas.

I just remember sitting on the couch that day. For hours...into the night. No one even turned on the light. I just sat there in the darkness, staring out the window, wondering if my father would come and rescue us.

Of course, he didn't.

When he first left my mother, he did stop by on a couple of occasions. He rented an apartment above a home up the street, and he would come by. He would fight with my mother and then try to pick fights with us. I think he was trying to joke around and make light of a serious divorce, but we never understood any of it. During this time, I would ride my little trike like a scooter with one foot on the seat and the other pushing myself off...real fast...to get away from him. I would envision myself in a rocket ship, moving at full speed in the opposite direction. Once, I got glass in my foot in the process.

He was very childish for an adult. We spent the night there a couple of times, but he didn't stay around long, and eventually, we just never heard from him again.

While we had some difficult moments like pets getting hit by a car on the busy road in front of our house, loud fights in the alley beside our home from living next door to a strip club, spending a lot of time alone while my mother worked, getting picked on, etc., the good outweighed the bad growing up.

I have many good memories of my childhood. I remember little tidbits, rarely whole memories. I recall my mother coming to get me from my grandparent's house after work (they lived across the alley from us my entire childhood), opening a bag, and a kitten jumping out. Or swinging on my grandparents' porch swing and picking cherries off of their cherry tree.

I spent a lot of time sitting with my elderly neighbors on their porch swings. They had so much wisdom, and I learned a lot from them. One lived beside us on the other half of our duplex, and the other lived behind us. We all shared the same yard. I would go between my grandmother's house to each of their homes. They would all give me candy.

Sometimes, I would spend hours at each of my neighbors' homes, not even talking, just sitting in silence or watching TV with them. Sometimes, they would talk to me about many different things. They would talk about life, events happening, who to trust, and who to stay clear of. We had a neighbor who would dig through our yard and find worms to sell once it started getting dark. Even though he scared me sometimes, they would tell me he was harmless. My brother is intellectually handicapped, and so was this neighbor (they were in a bowling league together), and I had to get used to some of his habits and way of talking with and interacting with people. His jokes seemed scary sometimes, but soon, I realized he was safe. Houses were very close together in our neighborhood, and we basically all shared this little city block.

My neighbors would crochet with me, play dolls with me, feed me, and fix me up when I hurt myself...they always knew when I was upset, even when I didn't tell them. And they would soothe me. They knew my father left and life was hard for my mother. They were so appreciated by me and mostly by my mother.

While my mother worked, my brother and I spent a great deal of time at my grandparent's house, too. They were the backbone of our family. They took me and my brother to many places as children: to visit family in other cities, to the lake, to Pirates' baseball games. My mother never had a vehicle once my father left, so if we ever traveled, it was typically with my grandparents since they had a car. If we ever needed to go anywhere any other time, we would either walk or take the city bus.

My grandmother never worked, except for a very small, part-time cleaning job for a radio station. She never had a driver's license so she would walk there. My grandfather always walked to and from work as well. He drove the city bus, so the car rarely left the yard. Nonetheless, it was a thrill when we went somewhere with them. It didn't matter if there was no A/C, and we sweated bullets every time we got in. There was a radio and a hand crank to put my window down, and that was enough for me.

My grandparents held dinner at their home every Sunday to bring the family together. Family was very important to them. I never understood why because most of the time, the family didn't get along. A lot of the family moved away, so it was really just my uncle, who lived with my grandparents most of his life and never had kids (until later in his life), and us. It was a treat when other family members were able to join us for dinner! My grandfather did most of the cooking, and his favorite dish was liver and onions. That was certainly not my favorite, so on those days, I didn't eat much. And got scolded for it. But Sunday was still my favorite day of the week. Even though we were all at different places in our lives and held different beliefs, making for very entertaining conversations at dinner, we still had family love. Ain't nothing like it!

———

I wasn't normal in a typical sense, but I wanted to be accepted. I had dreams and aspirations like most kids did my age. I learned to play the violin in elementary school and continued to play it up until graduation day. I rarely picked it up after that. But I spent my entire childhood in orchestra class. At first, I used my mother's old violin from when she was a child. I am pretty sure I still have it. And then, in middle school, my mother took out a payment plan for me to get a really nice violin once I outgrew that one.

I loved playing the violin! I could get lost in classical music. I could demonstrate my emotions through the dynamics of the notes. I could go from piano (soft) to forte (loud) and even to pizzicato (when you don't touch your bow to your string but instead pluck the string with your finger). I felt my heart come alive with every stroke of my bow. Sometimes, I would get so nervous during performances, but then as I got into it, I would get lost in the music and wouldn't even remember I was performing!

To add on, I also sang alto in the choir at school, starting in elementary school, where I played Baby Bop in my fifth-grade play. I loved it because I was in a costume, so no one even knew it was me. I could really get into it when no one could pick on me but instead wanted to get their photo with me afterward. I don't sing much in my adult years, and I sooooo miss singing. The feeling of transforming my voice with crescendos and decrescendos, a good pause for exaggeration and intensity, vibratos and harmonies, and so much magic. My joy comes in harmonizing with other voices. Solo performances are great, but when two or more voices combine, creating a beautiful unity, I just think that is wizardly.

I twirled a flag in both indoor guard and color guard, so I could attend football games to participate in the half-time shows. I think I miss attending football games the most in regards to being out of school. There was so much magic in the band and colorguard, intertwining in choreography together on the field. But now, I am able to attend sporting events that my children participate in.

High school was hard for me. When I was sixteen, I guess I had my first boyfriend experience, and it was awful! I lost my virginity. I didn't want to. I was scared! I kept saying no, that I wasn't ready. He kept pressuring me until I silently gave in. After it started, I said stop. It was so painful! But he never stopped until he was done.

<u>No Means NO!!</u>
I said I was scared.
I said I wasn't ready,
I wasn't prepared.
I said no, and I meant it.
No means no.

I told you,
I've never done this before.
I don't know what I'm doing.
I cried on the floor...
I've heard it was painful.
I was trembling.
I looked away.
That means no, too.

When I was silent,
With no more answers to give,
I was not suggestive
That you could penetrate.
I wanted to wait
I was unwilling.

I gave no consent,
I just stopped resisting.
I ran out of reasons,
You wouldn't stop, and you entered.

At that point,
I gave up the fight.
But please don't mistake,
It still wasn't right.
You kept on going
Until you had finished.

I tried to stop you.
I told you it hurt.
I should have been more assertive.
I should have been louder.
Oh, how I wish I was stronger than that.

My first time was supposed to be special
But it was taken from me.
It was nowhere near how I planned it to be.
I lost my voice and all of my choices.
No means no!!

Whether in word or in action.
I said no that day—
Multiple times, in so many ways.
No means no, and I meant it.

And now those who enter my life after you
Will likely be the ones to pay.
As my choices become harder than they have to be.

As I push them away.
I won't let them near me
And who knows how long I'll be that way.
But I will make sure
They understand
That no means no when I mean it.

I had such little self-worth, I went along with it. I now know that it is okay to change your mind. If you give in, then want to stop, allow yourself to stop. Don't continue in fear.

I do believe fathers play a vital role in many phases of development, especially when it comes to girls. I lost out on a lot of life lessons, like how a man should treat a woman, what boundaries I should set with men, emotional security, stability, how to interact appropriately with people, my expectations of them, and even my love and acceptance of myself. At this particular point in my life, I possibly had some abandonment issues that I hadn't worked through yet. I hadn't needed to work through them up until this point since it was my first sexual relationship.

Because I had a hunger to be accepted and loved, I think this desire clouded my judgment in some of the decisions I made, and especially during this first encounter. I am not implying that he was some type of predator or something. I just had a hard time being clear and direct. I exuded characteristics that screamed *"use me!" Abuse me! I deserve it! And if I cry **"stop,"** don't stop...it's not even about me, it's about you, so don't worry about me...* I am not justifying what went down that day. But I acknowledge I struggled with communicating my wants and needs. I play things off. I smile a lot like I am not bothered, and I did so with a shrug afterwards. And he could have mistaken my pleas because I wasn't firm in the least.

He will deny that I cried, or that I begged him to stop, but the truth is, when a man who feels the need to have power over you can't control you any longer, he will try to control how others see you. He will try to isolate you and turn people against you. He will tell people you are lying and that your reality didn't really happen. And that is what happened. I confided in a few people and they told me he said I was lying. I didn't have confidence, and I didn't have the fight, so I became withdrawn.

This experience, mixed with the fact that I grew up without a father, paved the way to my future decisions in regards to love and self-worth...

There was a time when I was sixteen or seventeen that my mother had a boyfriend. He started trying to help me study for my driving test, which I didn't end up taking until I was eighteen. It was my uncle from California who ultimately stepped in and helped me obtain my license by driving all the way to Pennsylvania to let me use his car. But nonetheless, her boyfriend played a role in me eventually getting my driver's license.

In certain moments, it was nice to have someone step into a fatherly position. My mother's boyfriend was around a lot and I could go to him with problems or when I needed advice. He took advantage of some of my life situations, like the horrible first intimate encounter I had with a boy that left me so fragile. He started asking to photograph me. He instilled in me this crazy idea that maybe I could model at the time. Weird, right? Since I wasn't exactly model material at that age...

So I allowed him to take some photos. My mother's boyfriend started making other subtle moves. It started with gaining my trust with all of these things he was focused on helping me with.

But then, he got weirder and began taking photos of me in a bikini. And then, offering me money in exchange for letting him touch me. It was uncomfortable, but he knew we didn't have money and that the reason I was interested in modeling was for money to save up for my future. I never touched him, and I didn't understand the things he would ask for. It never turned to sex. I always just let him touch my breast for a second and then would throw my shirt down and run out of the house. It really creeped me out, and I was so relieved when my mother said they broke up. I didn't tell her about it until later in my adult life, and when she asked him about it, he told her I was eighteen. That definitely wasn't true. But the conversation with my mother ended there. At this time in my life, I really struggled with self-worth and put up with some really stupid shit.

Like, really stupid, uncomfortable shit.

The last piece of my story that kind of created this perfect storm for the next chapter of my life was the passing of my grandmother, the glue of our family.

This story really started when my grandfather had a heart attack just a couple of months before my grandmother was diagnosed with colon cancer. He was admitted into a nursing home with other heart complications. He was paralyzed and lost all short-term memory, reverting back to when he was a bus driver. My grandmother tried to visit him as much as possible, but she fell very ill very quickly. Right before I graduated high school, she passed away. He attended her funeral, where my mother and I sang a duet together, and he cried, saying how beautiful it was. I don't think he understood that she was gone. He went back to the nursing home, yelling her name in the hallway every day, over and over, just looking for her and waiting for her to come see him.

Even though I didn't have a father figure, my grandfather could always sense that I was craving that male authority and comfort in my life. He would take me on "dates" to McDonald's in his old car. He would order what I wanted. Actually, he would order what he wanted me to have because there seemed to be a necessary respect for his male position. I was always told never to speak back at him, so I was never allowed to say, "no onions." Anyway, he did hold open doors for me, pull out my chair, and he would tell me to never settle for less. Why didn't I listen?

I left my hometown a couple days after graduation, and besides the short time I went back to live in necessity, I rarely made it back to visit. I saw my grandfather a couple times in those years before he passed away. He called me by my mother's name. When I was eighteen years old, my mother had a baby (my little brother). And anytime my younger brother was visiting my grandfather, he would call him by his youngest son's name (my uncle).

He would think he was driving his city bus while strolling up and down the hallway in his wheelchair and would say, "Are you getting on or aren't you?" Oh, what I wouldn't do to get behind him and push his wheelchair one more time as I said, "Of course I am getting on this bus."

My last time seeing him was at his funeral when my firstborn was only a couple of months old. He never even got to meet him. I have a hard time processing my feelings and don't like the thought of goodbye, so I particularly have a hard time at funerals.

Putting a lot of effort into my school work paid off when I completed high school because I graduated third in my class of 221 students. What an accomplishment! I then really started thinking and worrying about my future and what I would do with my life. The only thing I knew was that I wouldn't be staying there. Johnstown, Pennsylvania, was a very small, depressing town. Always has been, and still is. It really became utterly desolate when my grandmother passed away, and I felt it was very important to pen how I felt during this awfully mournful time.

<u>Your Spirit Lives On</u>
Staring out of my window,
I feel such insufferable heartbreak...
Unbearable dejection...
As I digest what just happened.

Today, I said goodbye to you.
Your physical body will never be seen again.
The casket closed, and you were lowered and buried in the dirt.
From dirt you came,
To dirt you returned.
Your body will no longer roam this earth,
But yet you remain.

You are the soft whispers,
gently caressing the towering weeping willow tree.
The drooping branches dance and sway, as you quietly cry out.
Your silent sobs echo in the night.
I feel you weep.

You are the wind that encircles me everywhere I go.
You sing songs of sweetness...songs of sorrow...
Songs that shout what my heart is trying to reveal.

You are the eagle that soars high above me.
Watching me.
Guiding me through this life of uncertainty.

You are the cardinal that looks in with patience
at my windowsill.

Peacefully telling me that it's okay to descend into my feelings,
As long as I don't stay there. As long as I rise again.
You guard me while I sleep.

You are the dove of tranquility.
You beautifully contrast against the darkness of the night sky.
You calm my spirit.
You subdue my soul.

You twinkle radiantly,
looking down at me in my world of loneliness.
You are the stars and the moon that light my way
As I travel down this road of dubitation.

You are the sun that allows my spirit to rise,
and you catch my fallen, shattered soul in your brilliant rays.
You give me warmth through the cold dark days.
You comfort me through the pain of losing you.

You tap quietly against my window pane.
You wash away my doubt and drown out my fears.
You are the rain that eventually creates a beautiful rainbow.
You restore me because, without rain, my soul would be dry...
bare...deserted...
You bring me back to life.

I see you in your robe of white, your crown of gold,
Your suffering is gone and you are finally free,
Wandering the earth, in everything I touch and see.
I see you in all of life's glory.
Your spirit lives on...

My grandmother's passing was the beginning of the end of my self-worth—what little I might have had. She was my place of comfort. And she would always tell me that I can be whoever I wanted to be, and reinforced that all throughout my life. Furthermore, she would say it was too late for her but never too late for me. She had a shaky arm. I think she told me it was because she broke her arm on her way out of the womb, and I think she sometimes felt defeated over that, but it never stopped her.

She practically raised me. Yes, my grandfather and I were close, but there was no bond like I had with my grandmother. Her quick passing was hard on all of us. At the end, she couldn't talk with tubes down her throat, but she penned out on a piece of paper asking us to pull the plug, because she was ready to go. And shortly after, she let go...

My biggest fear kept happening over and over in life. I was forcefully isolated—deserted, whether intentionally or not. Important people in my life left or didn't treat me well and I let it define me. I started building this wall around me, trying to find any type of control over my life I could. I became withdrawn and unsettled. During this time, I decided to find peace from within. When I felt like everyone around me was disappointing me, I began to make it a mission to trust and rely on myself. I began to coexist with myself and found that I am actually quite savage.

When my grandmother left, I felt extremely lost. I couldn't wait to leave that town and start over. I truly thought this was the lowest I could possibly get. I felt like I was allowing these traumas to define me and just knew everyone was looking at me in shame by judging me and my loneliness. What came next was so much harder than I ever thought life could be.

Self-Reflection:

1. When you are going through a hard time, is there something that you do to get through it? If you haven't been introduced to coping skills that work for you yet, what is something you enjoy doing that offers you an escape from reality so you can get past hard moments? For most of my life, that thing was writing poetry. I think we all find an escape somewhere. In art, in music, in penning our thoughts. Dig deep and find that warrior—that overcomer inside just dying to come out. How can you tap into that part of yourself that allows you to feel empowered?

____

____

____

____

____

____

2. Do you feel like there are moments of trauma in your life that you have allowed to define you? Take a piece of paper and write down some of those moments. How can you get past them? Once you have reflected on this and have written down not only traumatic moments you allowed to define you but also ways to get past them, work on getting yourself through it. Don't rush this. You can get through this list in a day or it may take a year. Put your burden and your list of ways to overcome it in a place where you can see and keep track.

____

____

____

____

____

____

3. Once you have completed your list, burn this paper and release it into the ether. Be free from the bondage you have allowed to take over. As soon as you check off that last item and you feel the burden lifted from you, burn! To me, this feels fierce, maybe a little primitive, but definitely SAVAGE!

____

____

____

____

____

____

chapter 2

THOU SHALT NOT TURN TO ADDICTION INSTEAD OF SELF

From the time of my first intimate encounter until the time I graduated high school, I made many awful decisions in regard to boys. I began turning to sex thinking it was making me feel better about myself. I thought, *I have to be good, whatever "good" means, if these guys like me, right?*

Maybe it was that I felt power over my life when I could make these sexual decisions when it seemed my life was out of control. Maybe I was trying to talk myself into loving myself. Maybe I just really craved the attention and affection and didn't care how it made me look or feel afterward, because I really did feel bad after the fact. But it was like an addiction. Not in a "take over my life" kind of way, but in a way that I felt like I needed it when I felt unworthy in order to show myself I was still adequate.

My greatest romantic experience was dating a foreign exchange student from Sweden. He was as close to respectful as I ever found in my younger years. He held doors open for me, he kissed my hand, and pulled out chairs. Even though we never saw each other again after he went back to Sweden, I do believe he saved me. He showed me what I needed to look for in my next relationships, and he paved the way for where I am right now, even though I made more mistakes in between.

A Better Version of Me
When you entered my life,
I was broken and battered.
Yet I slowly let you inside.

You came from so far away,
And you brought out the best in me,
I needed you in that moment.

I enjoyed my time with you.
You showed me how I should be treated.
I remember the goodness inside of you,
The love in your eyes,
The kindness in your touch.
The happiness you brought me.

When it was time for you to go back home,
I didn't quite understand our last days together.
I'm sure it was a defense
To make the transition easier.

Looking back, God had a plan.
It was all supposed to happen that way.
For you were just a stepping stone
To prepare me for where I am today.

For that, I will always forever be grateful
You paved the way
For me to see my inner-worth

So that I could show it to the world.
You have helped me create
A better version of me.

When he left, I had that weird period where my mother's boyfriend was taking advantage of my crushed spirit, but once I was able to get through and past that, I took a long pause from anything that had to do with the male species.

Up until this point, life just molded me. My experiences dictated my responses and my actions. I knew I wanted better for myself, and I knew I needed help. I soon realized, however, that I had to help myself.

Just a couple of short days after I graduated high school, I left for the military, a spur-of-the-moment decision out of desperation. A few recruiters visited my school throughout my senior year. I grabbed a pamphlet once but never put much thought into it. My uncle, who lived in California, was in the Marines, but none of my local family had any connection to the military.

If you recall, my grandmother passed away right before I graduated and that was probably the biggest reason I made this quick decision to join the Army. I didn't prepare; I didn't even have a chance to tell many people I was leaving. I left very quickly and quietly.

I primarily signed up for the military because of the promise of free college. I didn't know what I was going to do with my life at that moment, but I knew I wanted to do something better than what I was currently doing. I scored well on the ASVAB (Armed Services Vocational Aptitude Battery) test when forced to take it in high school. So at that moment, I figured, what could I lose?

Perhaps my sudden decision to leave in this manner was prompted by my need for an escape, or maybe I found this fight inside that I learned from my mother. Either way, I didn't know then when I made this life-changing decision that this would be the basis of who I am today.

I learned so much throughout my time in the military, but the majority of my findings came from basic training at Fort Jackson, South Carolina, and AIT (Advanced Individual Training) held at Fort Lee, Virginia.

A lot has happened from the time I left for the Army until now that has led me to the life I currently live, and I owe it all to this one act of stepping out of my comfort zone to do what I needed to do to save myself.

But while I was in training, I just knew they were going to break me! It was the hardest experience of my young life. If it didn't break me physically, I just knew it would break me mentally! I went in at 118 lbs and 5'5" tall. I couldn't even do one pushup.

I cried almost every night. The experience was too much for me to handle most times, though I couldn't show that. During training, if one person messed up, the entire platoon paid for it. We didn't get much sleep. We were woken abruptly in the middle of the night, often, for punishment in the form of physical fitness. We would have to do forced pushups (aka getting dropped or what the military calls beating my face), planks, calf raises, leg lifts, and many other different moves that we would have to hold for long periods of time until we reached muscle failure. Once, we were doing these army crawls, and our female drill sergeant stomped on my fingers.

It was HOT in Jacksonville, South Carolina, and I had heat stroke during my stay there on one occasion. Once while going over a net wall, on my way down, I missed a step and fell to the ground. Turned out I had a hairline fracture in my left leg. I had the choice to get recycled and repeat basic training or complete my final PT (physical training) test. I was NOT going through that again, so somehow I finished my final test and passed with a broken leg. Boy, that was rough! But I got through!

I didn't have many people back home to write to and even lost a lot of friends when I decided to join the military. Mainly, it was because we just lost touch. And life back then isn't like it is now. There were no cell phones or laptops, no social media, and no real way to quickly get in touch with someone. Even when I wasn't at boot camp and was in the comfort of my own home, the computer systems were slow, and that AOL (America OnLine) dial-up sound is something I will never forget! Life was much-slower paced back then.

Once a week, we were able to wait in a long line and make calls home on a payphone. We could also write letters in the mail. Weeks later, we would get a response back. I did have just a couple of people I could count on to help me get through by sending me an occasional letter.

My time away at training allowed me to take a much-needed pause from the way I was living life. It allowed me to focus on myself—my physical and mental health, and I needed that. Or maybe I was so busy doing different tests, learning new skills, combat moves, and gas chambers, among other things, that I didn't have time to feel sorry for myself. I grew stronger. Every time I was faced with punishment I didn't think I could handle, I pushed myself and I got through it. As a result, it built my confidence.

I was a marksman at the shooting range, something I never thought I would ever do. I didn't think through any of this when I joined the Army. But there I was, killing it and shit.

It really was a spur-of-the-moment decision and one I will never regret.

<u>The Army</u>
I went in weak,
Mentally, physically, emotionally,
I was broken.

I struggled with the physical pain.
I couldn't hold myself up.
I reached muscle failure daily.

I struggled in my mind.
I cried each night for the first few weeks.
I felt alone and brittle.

I had already gone through so much.
I wasn't prepared.
But day by day,
My mentality strengthened.

Within no time, I conquered my thoughts.
I overcame my weaknesses.
I told myself, "I WILL do this."
And I did.

After basic training in South Carolina, I went to Virginia for educational military training. Here, I learned how to do the job I was assigned to do. My MOS (Military Occupational Specialty) was 92A-Automated Logistical Specialist, so I handled work in the motor pool. I dispatched vehicles, created driver's licenses for military vehicles, ordered parts, and much more.

During this time, I mainly had classroom studies throughout the day and some free time in the evenings. It had a slightly different feel than basic training, but we still had physical

punishment if we didn't do the right thing. We still had forma-
tions at certain times, platoon marches to the chow hall, physical
training in the mornings, and many routines familiar from basic
training. However, it was more mental work than physical.

But still, I left training at 134 pounds of pure muscle, in the
best shape of my life, because I told myself I could. My best friend
from high school showed up for me at the Greyhound station
when I made it back from training. That meant so much to me...

I did have a crush on a guy at AIT, but he didn't give me the
time of day. Ha! Disaster averted there, I suppose. I also hung out
with another guy, but it wasn't serious in an emotional kind of
way. And that was after many months of not having any interest
in anyone and just working on getting myself together. I was
happy to have had this opportunity for emotional solitude. Frat-
ernization was not allowed in the military, so a forced hiatus was
kind of a breath of fresh air.

When I came back to my mother's home after I graduated
from both boot camp and AIT, I met my little brother. It was so
weird being 19 years old with a newborn brother.

I had a couple of months off and then began attending my
weekend drills, as I was in the Army Reserves. There, I met my
ex-husband.

We dated and were having fun. It started feeling rushed
pretty quickly, however. I didn't want to bring him to my home
because we didn't have much money, and frankly, I was embarrassed. I didn't like going to his house because I felt like I couldn't
be myself there. His parents were great, but they lived differently
than I did. They seemed to have their shit together, and I felt
judged a lot, whether that was their intention or not.

He lived with his mom and stepdad and had lived through
his parents divorcing, so he related to me somewhat. That was
nice and such a comfort to me. Because we didn't like going to

each other's homes, we spent a lot of time out and even slept in either his car or my car many times. So when he asked me to move to Virginia because he wanted to attend Liberty University, I said, "Sure, why not!!" I've always had a wild spirit anyway, so this sounded fun!

We married shortly after moving into our small apartment together because he said his family was very against us living together and not being married. I really thought getting married was a new start for me. I thought, *Finally, someone loves me.* Reality was much different than that, however. Our wedding day was the beginning of the end for us.

We got married in Pennsylvania at the church my mother attended. It was a nice, small, quaint wedding. It was all we could afford. He wore his military uniform, and I was content that day, but our connection started diminishing well before this day of marriage.

Shortly after getting married, my ex-husband started treating me differently. Or I felt different. I'm not sure if it was him or me. I worked, but my jobs were very part-time, so I didn't bring in nearly as much money as he did. He made sure I understood that he had an upper hand over me, that he made all of the money and had control. He would make comments in a seemingly joking way that he believed women should be submissive. And silent. He became distant.

As he became disconnected, I became overly mistrustful of what he was doing when he wasn't with me. These feelings within me probably drew a further wedge between us. Jealousy isn't a good feeling at all. After all, I had left my small town that held all of my family and what little friends I had and followed him to another state where I knew no one. I grew dependent on him since he was the only person I knew in a new place.

Soon, we bought a home together. I got to know the neighbors and really enjoyed spending time with them. They had Doberman pinscher dogs who guarded the property as we shared a driveway. Their mother lived behind our home, and I really enjoyed going to her home to crochet and hang out with her. When my husband was away, I spent as much time there as I possibly could because I didn't like being home alone.

Maybe this hatred of being alone stemmed from just spending so much time in what felt like solitude while going through military training. At that moment in my life, I had had enough alone time.

We did some really stupid things—one that comes to mind is hooking up with another couple, where he ended up getting drunk and trying to sleep with the wife alone. That opened the door to us breaking our vows. But the truth is that our marriage was over way before this. And this was the moment I realized addiction is a lifelong battle. I didn't comprehend at that moment that I assisted in ending our marriage by suggesting we get cozy with another couple to fulfill my intimate needs when I should have sought them in him alone.

After only a few short months of being married, he took a full-time military job several hours away, leaving me at home. There wasn't really a discussion about it. He voluntarily took a tour in Northern Virginia, and I took this as a signal that he wanted to be away from me. For some reason, that is always where my mind went when he didn't want to be home.

When it came to saving the marriage, I tried to make it work but was unsuccessful. I drove up to spend time with him and cook for him as he lived with roommates. I don't even like to cook! And after a bit of time, I started falling into a deep depression. When I went there, I always felt like the third wheel. He would hang out with his roommates and act like a bachelor. I felt invisible...

Occasionally, he would come home to visit. Those times were nice. We took day trips and outings. I really enjoyed those efforts and longed to have more times like those.

I've always known that I wanted to be a mother. I had dreamed of it for so long, but at that point, I didn't have any children. I would spend a lot of time treating our dog as if she were my child. I would bake dog biscuits, and she would sleep in my bed. We picked her out together, and she instantly bonded and guarded both of us.

She was loving at just the right moments. She was playful and fun. I didn't know I needed her until she entered my life. We went places together and took walks. She gave me a reason to get out of the house and provided a great distraction from my husband being gone. She filled a void.

One awful day, she ran out the door and down our long driveway. Our screen door never latched shut. I was getting ready to get in the shower when I heard her outside barking, so I threw my robe on and ran out the door. Imagine a large German shepherd on the side of the road, running up and back as each car drove past. She would run behind a car and escape the next car just in time to get behind it, beginning the chase all over again. It was a game to her. Just as I would coax her to me, another car would pass, and she would go right back to chasing, barely escaping her fate.

Sadly, one driver just wasn't paying attention, or maybe he intentionally hit her...right in front of me just as she was heading back in my direction. I believe she died instantly, blood running from her nose and eyes. It was the most horrifying thing I had ever witnessed! I ran to the house to get clothes on (as I was just in a bathrobe), and when I came back, she was gone.

That thought of *I know she couldn't have made it through that hard hit, but maybe she walked away alive! I must find her!* turned into *There's no way she survived this, but where is she?* I wandered the woods all around our home trying to find her. When it started getting dark, I headed back to the house.

I then took to making phone calls, trying different shelters and vet hospitals. I finally reached someone the next morning and learned that a person who witnessed her getting hit had taken her to the closest animal hospital where she had passed prior to arrival. I began to greatly hate the situation I was in. I was lonely, my husband wasn't around, and my only companion was gone. I had no one to help me through this moment. I had only myself to lean on.

Tragedy

My family, my child. So what, you had fur?
I loved you as if you were.
As if I gave birth to you.
We ate at the table, you slept in my bed.
How could someone just leave you for dead?

You got me through dark nights, lonely days.
Made me happy in so many ways.
My companion, protector, loyal, always by my side.
Until that day you broke outside.

You pushed through the crack and charged down the drive
Your bark so loud, so vivid in my mind.
You thought it was a game, chasing each car that passed
Then just like that
You were taken from me...

I'll never forget the sound of that machine
Colliding with your body, gone instantly

The sight of blood seeping from your nose and eyes
Oh, how I cried and cried...
The most horrible thing I had ever been through
Stolen from me. I needed you.

What a tragedy to ever get through.
Tori, I love you.

Soon after my furry companion passed away, I learned I was pregnant. For a very brief moment, we went from shock to worry about how we would be able to afford a baby, to a little bit of hope that maybe we could make our marriage work, even if just for the sake of the baby (terrible idea, by the way). We also got a basset hound puppy in hopes that I would have another companion while my husband was away.

He returned from his tour, and things intensified. We didn't really know how to communicate. It was toxic and miserable. He drank; I cried and screamed. At one point, it got physical. I don't think he meant to hurt me. I think he was trying to keep me from hurting myself and would pin me to keep me from doing what I was threatening to do, which was always directed towards myself.

And a short time later, I lost our baby.

At that point, I had had enough. I was lonely, and he was lonely. He was seeing someone, and I had started seeing someone, too. I would talk to men online. I even had a moment where I drove to Pennsylvania and was hanging out with someone from my younger years. He drove back with me to Virginia. I think he wanted to protect me. But there was no plan and when we got back to Virginia, I had no idea what to do next, so I bought him a ticket back home on the Greyhound. I don't think we talked again after that, but each moment in my life led me to the next, and I feel like every step happened for a reason.

My uncle drove to Virginia to pick me up, and we took a road trip back to California where I stayed a little while before getting on a plane back home to make some serious decisions. During this trip, I saw the Grand Canyon and other beautiful places in this country. This isn't the first time my uncle distracted me. As a teenager, he took my brother and I on a road trip to Niagara Falls to get away. I credit a lot of my love of traveling to him.

Upon my return, I realized I didn't want the life I was living, and I began doing things to dull my feelings. I drank. I started cutting myself. Outside pain seemed to take away my internal pain. Or so I told myself. I felt like I had control over my internal struggles for the first time in my life. Just like my tattoos tell a story of my life, so do my scars. At one point, I got a tattoo to put over my wrist scars. That in itself tells a story of the shame I felt every time I did it.

But as much as I liked to think the things I was doing gave me power over myself, they kind of took over me. I needed help. I saw a doctor and was prescribed antidepressants. After spending a month in my bed crying over the loss of my first baby, my ex-husband and I had a huge fight. When I superficially cut my wrist with a butterknife, trying to seek his attention, he called the cops, and they took me to Virginia Baptist Hospital, where they forced me to check myself in.

This was the first step to getting help. Even though it was forced, I am so thankful.

In the Stillness
Lying in complete darkness,
The silence breaks me down.
In isolation, I cry alone.

The stillness hard to bear,
I'm consumed in my emptiness.
This motionless, soundless, lifeless place.
Dormant, hibernative state.
Forcefully sedated.

Softly slumbered state of mind,
Contemplated cessation a thousand times.
Instead, I just paused,
Proceeded with a commanded coma,
Just to be able to seek
Order and control in my life.
I find comfort in the pause.

I find rest in the desist.
I seek peace while unmoving,
As the world around me turns.

Once I arrived at the hospital, I was placed on different anti-depressants and medications, so I don't remember much of my stay there. I do remember having a conversation with the police and getting a restraining order on my husband. At that moment, I never wanted to see him or talk to him again because he put me there. He made the decision to have me committed instead of empathizing with me and all that I had been through. He chose again to separate from me and left me alone to deal with my pain.

I remember, after a couple days of being there and calming down from my angry state, spending a lot of my time by the pay phone, trying to call him. The phone would just ring and ring most times. When he did answer, he repeatedly told me that losing the baby was the best thing for us because we couldn't afford it, and he kept telling me that his parents were advising him that he needed to leave me.

I spent a lot of the time in the hospital sedated. I'm sure they made me go through group and individual therapy. I'm sure it helped. I can't tell you; I don't remember much.

I questioned God a lot during this time of my life, but He knew what He was doing. He strategically placed these hardships in my path in order to mold me. He sometimes damn near broke me in order to fix me up just the way He wanted me or needed me to be. You see, God uses broken people to do His work. It is all a part of His master plan! Therefore, I needed to go down the roads I went down, and I needed to face what I faced. I didn't understand it as I was making this journey, but looking back, it is now so clear. But in that moment, all I felt was defeat.

Once I checked myself out of the hospital, my neighbor came to pick me up and told me that my husband was having women stay at my house while I was gone. I remember not even feeling mad about it. I had nowhere to go, but then the family I babysat for was kind and allowed me to stay in their basement for some time.

As I recall, one day, my ex-husband told me I could come by and pick up some of my belongings because I only had a few items in hand. This time period is a bit of a blur, but I remember showing up and him calling the cops. I was arrested for breaking a restraining order. At that moment, I didn't even know he had a restraining order on me. I thought, *Why would he do that? I didn't threaten him, I was only threatening harm to myself!* That's what led to me going to the hospital. As they were taking me away in handcuffs, I was asking so many questions. "Why is this happening? I didn't do anything wrong. I just needed some of my belongings. What restraining order?" But they didn't want to hear any of it.

I spent a week in jail.

There were no cells for me because the jail was overcrowded. I felt like I was being kicked while I was already down. I was completely alone. That was the lowest point in my entire life. That moment right there. In jail. On the cold floor. Alone.

No shower, no contact with anyone I knew, a week of isolation. Another forced pause.

I had no one. I just had to wait my time until the court date they set, which was a week later. A woman inside who was twice my age really helped me. I wasn't even in there long enough to be able to order shampoo or anything. On the day of the hearing, she allowed me to use hers so I could clean myself up a little. Of course, I looked like absolute shit because I had been crying the entire week and asking myself over and over how the hell I ended up there. Not just in jail but asking myself, *How did I end up at such a low place?*

At the court hearing, charges were dropped—but that week in jail was hell. It was enough to help me realize that I needed to get myself out of the situation I was in. Even though the worst was over by this point, it was such a hard time for me. I was my own worst enemy, and being inside my own head was the darkest place I had ever been in my life. But to be honest, I am not sure I would have had the strength to up and leave the situation had I not been FORCED to pause.

I lived in my car for a few days, and then my ex-husband left for a tour in Iraq. Just before he left, I was finally coming to grips with the fact that he was toxic for me. He was seeing someone who went with him to Iraq, and I decided to let go and move on. I found homes for our pets (we had our basset hound, a cat, and a potbelly pig), packed up the very little I had into my trunk, and moved to Ohio.

What hurt me the most about the breakup was his utter

disrespect for me and what was important to me. Because I was carried to jail, I never had the opportunity to get any of my belongings. While I was in jail, he threw away everything, including the sewing machine my grandmother had given to me —the last item I had to remember her by...

Just to show you the damage done to the inside of me, here is a poem I wrote directly after I made the decision to leave.

In Despair
Spirit crushed
Heart shattered
Life over
Nothing matters
Mind restless
Body trembling
Numb all over
Dull aching
In complete despair

At this point, I went through a phase of promiscuity. Of course I did. It was my way of feeling self-sufficient, even though I was actually the opposite of that. In my mind, I was handling my needs by finding a way to feel good, but the truth is that I only felt good when someone said yes to me and satisfied me. And then, that feeling good turned to feeling bad and ashamed.

Every. Single. Time.

I left to go to Ohio for a summer job at Cedar Point (an amusement park) where I worked at the petting farm. My best friend, the one who met me at the Greyhound station when I got home from basic training, went with me. I thought this would give me a chance to start over. It was a great opportunity. I had free housing and shared a dorm with about a dozen other women working there. And there was this deal that, if I stayed the entire term of my contract, I would earn an extra dollar for every hour I worked and receive a bonus check at the end. It gave me the opportunity to save a little, which I wouldn't have done on my own.

This was another pause before my next move. But I didn't use it for the time I needed for myself. I drank and drank that summer. Someone even stole my engagement ring out of my purse at the bar, which I used to carry around to remind myself of where I was and where I have been in life.

Sadly, I can't remember much about that summer. As I said earlier, a common theme for my life. One night, I remember going in and out of consciousness in a boy's dorm. I had bruises all over me the next day. I am pretty sure I was drugged that night, and who knows how many other nights that summer. I don't recall most of it. I suppose it was just my way of trying to get through such a hard time in my life.

I Find Solace in the Bottle

I'm alone...my thoughts are scattered.
I'm afraid...
I ache as I realize,
I never mattered...

The shit in this bottle helps me forget...
How disarranged my life has been since we met.

Just months after our vows were bound,
He ABANDONED me...
He took a job away from home,
Almost a year, I was left wanting...
Overpowered by loneliness.

Around the time he returned, I discovered I was pregnant...
And within a short time, I grievously miscarried.

The mental abuse, the fateful force...
My despondency worst.
I had to leave, I could not stay.
I surrendered, I had to go away.

If I didn't, I would have collapsed.
I would have stumbled...
Succumbed to my hopelessness...
Accepted my sorrow.
But instead, I'm surviving, by tipping the bottle.

Each day that passes, I slowly forget about my inner affliction,
With each drink I swallow,
I find solace in the bottle.

I left Ohio with the guy I was seeing from Cedar Point, and we moved to Charlottesville, Virginia, where we took on a job opportunity on a Rottweiler farm. There, we stayed in a small RV on the property.

When we were at Cedar Point, he fulfilled my needs there. He was very clingy, and I guess I needed that. I needed to feel wanted by someone. At the time, I in no way wanted to be tied down to anyone. As much as he tried, it wasn't for me. One of the items on my list of stupid things I've done in life was get a tattoo of a tadpole (his name was Tadd) down by my secret place. I later tattooed over it with a tribal rose, warrior that I am.

One day as I was out looking for a vehicle, I met my son's father. He was a car salesman and sold me my first brand-new car. I was still living with the guy from Ohio at the time, but we weren't romantically involved and were both in the process of trying to find other living situations.

I finally found an apartment at a college house, where I shared a living space with a couple of other women. I pretty much kept to myself, but my time there was nice. I found a stray kitten and named him Daniel. He occupied my time and fulfilled my needs during this stage of my life.

After just a few short months with the car salesman, I ended up pregnant. Once I told him that I was pregnant, we had no more contact. He decided if I would not get an abortion, he would have nothing to do with me or this baby. To this day, he has not seen his son, who is now almost an adult! But abortion was not an option for me.

Absolutely not. He is a part of me...

This is the point in my life where I decided to stop drinking. I didn't do it for myself. I did it for him. My baby boy that my body was nurturing and growing and providing for. He was innocent and deserved a chance at a good life. I vowed to do everything in my power to provide that for him.

One day, I got a phone call from a neighbor. They found Daniel, who was an indoor/outdoor kitty, and called the number on the tag. They said he had been hanging out there a lot and asked if he needed someone to care for him or if he was already cared for. This came at a perfect time in my life when I wasn't sure what was in store for me so I agreed for them to be his people.

I couldn't stay in a college dorm long with a baby coming, so I found a small studio apartment where I lived when my son was born. It was quaint and quiet, out in the country, way outside of town. It was cute and I loved being there because my landlord lived upstairs and he was kind. I also had awesome neighbors and really enjoyed the solitude I felt there. However, I didn't stay there long.

I delivered my baby all alone at the hospital. I had some complications, mainly just preeclampsia, and I delivered him in the middle of the night. Once labor started, it was pretty smooth and all went well. All was good, until it wasn't.

It didn't take me long to realize I was hitting some post-partum depression. I was having a hard time finding joy in my situation. My baby had colic, cried a lot, and I had no idea what to do to make him stop. The only thing that seemed to help was putting his seat on the dryer and turning it on. And sometimes, just taking a drive would ease him a bit. I guess the noise and movement lulled him to sleep.

I did a lot of driving at this time.

I got a bad infection when he was about a week old and had no one to care for him. I had to take him with me to the hospital and stay with me overnight while the nurses helped me with him. When I was released, I went back to not eating or sleeping and focusing only on taking care of this little bundle who solely depended on me. It was just him and me.

Him and me against the world!

Eventually, it got easier. However, the studio apartment got tight once my son started crawling and walking. I started dating someone from work, and I found a two-bedroom cottage. Just a couple doors down, I also found a babysitter for him.

My work friend soon decided to move in with us. Prior to this, my boss was hitting on me. After several advances and several times of saying no, I turned him in because I was feeling violated and trying to take back my life. I don't know what happened with that situation because just as my work friend and I were moving in together, we both got fired for fraternizing at work. I'm not sure if that was the real reason or if it was over turning in my boss for his unwanted advances, but it was a hard moment. I wasn't sure how I would get through this with all of these new responsibilities...

Notice the pattern?

But I made it through in better shape than before. My work friend got a social work position, and I took an accounting position at a car wash company with much better pay. Funny how things turn out.

Ironically, when my son turned a month old, I was turning a curve in the rain with bald tires. I flipped the car that my son's father sold me into a tree, totaling it. Luckily, my son didn't even have a scratch on him. I ended up having to get thirteen stitches in my butt cheek from trying to climb to the back to get to him. The sound of his cries that day is probably the best sound I have ever heard in my life.

<u>Allowing Me to Live Again</u>
Life could be so different now, but
I was spared
My son—my life—my everything.
On that night I was so scared.
The sound of your cries
Brought me to tears
Thinking of all your years to come
Your life to live
How much you have to give to the world
The stories to make
And on that rainy night, when my car aired
Into a tree
And someone stopped to check on you,
I wasn't thinking of me
I had to get to where you were

Once I saw you, the rest is blurred
And frankly doesn't matter.

I'm thankful it wasn't worse than it was
The car totaled but you, my son
Are able to grow up and live a good life
Whatever you determine that is.
Thank God for second chances
And a warning to:
Just.
Slow.
Down.
Especially in the rain.
In the dark and dreary times.
Pause. Breathe. And live again…

What I didn't mention is I crashed because I was arguing with the guy I was dating at the time. Things started getting weird towards the end of our relationship. Because I had been through this before, I knew the signs, and I knew what I didn't want. I didn't want someone telling me what to do. I didn't want someone making demands of me.

One night, I awoke to him being gone. I went looking for him to find him looking through my trash can in my car and piecing together a letter I had received, read, and thrown away. It was from a guy I used to date who was in jail. We weren't together any longer, and it had been years since I dated him (this was before I even joined the military). Yes, he gave me compliments, which is the reason I ripped the letter up, but I didn't respond to it. Not until much later, anyway.

Soon after, I found out I was pregnant. Just like the last pregnancy I miscarried and grieved. Because of the weirdness and mistrust at the end of the relationship, we just decided it was best to part ways. There was an odd period between breaking up and moving on when we had a hard time letting go. The miscarriage was bizarre, and it took over a month to get the pregnancy hormones down, giving the impression that maybe the baby was fighting and could beat this. But the hormone numbers slowly went down to zero. We did have a lot of chemistry, but ultimately, we both had a lot of growing up to do. And once the miscarriage was complete, so were we.

Another failed, fairly serious relationship. I was pretty disappointed at this point. My son was getting used to him and seemed to really care for him. I was starting to feel awful. How could I, a fatherless child, carry on the legacy by bringing a fatherless child into this world?

I embraced the task of raising my son on my own for a while. I didn't want to hurt him again by allowing someone else to come into my life and fill such an important role just to let him down. That is, until the summer of 2006. At that time, I was still up to my old habits. I was letting my addiction take over, still not willing to commit to anyone, and struggling with my self-worth. I started drinking again and ended up attending a summer annual training for my military obligation. During this two week period, I was promiscuous, drinking, and ended up pregnant with my daughter during a one-night stand.

Amazingly, this time, I wasn't alone during her delivery. A couple of friends from my car wash job and an old roommate from the college dorm came to help deliver her. It was amazing to feel support from friends.

At this point in my life, I was so conflicted. I saw the beauty in the world around me. I had good people in my life. There was a woman from the church I occasionally attended who even helped on several occasions by bringing me groceries! I had amazing support, and I so much appreciated those in my life at that moment in time. I had two amazing children who lit up my entire world...but still, I hadn't found that inner peace I so desperately needed. After all, I now had two fatherless children.

TWO!

I thought, *How can I do this after knowing what it has done to me?*

I felt sometimes like I wasn't even living. I was only coping. The thing about addiction and habits is that they are lifelong struggles to change and so, so hard to break. And once you start recovery, you work forever to maintain it. I'm very transparent to say a lot of my life is a blur. I don't remember a lot. Only bits and pieces.

I've heard people with PTSD and even grief at times often suffer from some type of memory loss. To be honest, I never even thought about it until I sat down to write this book and realized that I had some shit to work through. I honestly thought I was in the early stages of dementia or Alzheimer's. I've spent a lot of time just going through the motions of life. But here, at this stage of my life, something just clicked. I started realizing, *Maybe I won't find happiness in someone else. Maybe what I drink won't make me happy. Maybe I have to find happiness within myself.*

I learned recently that I get a high from the feeling of being overwhelmed. Because of this, I create scenarios to get this reaction within myself. I fill my schedule to the brink in order to get to this emotion. I have a desire to move every two years, to quit, and get a new job every two years. I don't know what it is about the two-year mark, but that is about the time I get the itch. Self-sabotage, maybe? Each time, it is for something better. For now, I am content with coping with this mechanism. Every time we move, we make a profit on our home. Every time I get a new job, I learn new skills and receive more pay. But I have been paying attention to this form of addiction I think I have had all throughout my life. And part of my process is being more self-aware.

Self-Reflection:

1. What addictions do you struggle with? Even good things can end up being addictions if you let them control your life. If you just have good habits—like you turn to exercise to help you get through a tough time, then that isn't an addiction. But if you are using exercise as a way of overcoming one thing, and then you exercise to the point of needing medical intervention, then it has become an addiction. Reflect more on some habits you may have that could be considered an addiction. Examine your life. Do you have specific patterns that always end up being your go-to when you are trying to get to a specific feeling or reaction within yourself? Really dig deep here. This is about self-awareness.

____

____

____

____

____

____

2. How can you overcome this addiction? For this self-reflection, I don't want you to burn and release to the ether like the last assignment. For this one, I want you to write ways you conquer that which overtakes you and put it somewhere you can see it often. The thing with addiction is it can be a lifelong struggle. You may feel like you have gotten through it, but then another

hard time comes upon you, and you turn to it again. So I want you to keep this in your view, somewhere you visit often. Attach it to your mirror in your bedroom or to the visor of your car. Once you find what helps you overcome it, turn to it again and again as needed.

soul-searching contractions

chapter 3

THOU SHALT TURN TO SELF IN HARD
TIMES

When I hit rock bottom, I started really looking internally. How could I have allowed myself to get to this point? How could I not remember a lot of my life? How could I put my kids in a situation where they were now fatherless children after going through it myself and letting that define my life for so long? I gave myself some grace, but *damnit, Jennifer.* To do the same damaging shit over and over, I really had a battle going on within myself.

<u>The Battle Within</u>
Filled with doubts, I close my eyes,
Choked by my own sobs and cries,
I bring it on myself, you know.
For I was hurt not so long ago
But I wear a good disguise.

Outwardly I seem okay,
But inside I face chaos.
I wrestle with myself.
No one can see through me.

I wear a smile, I pitch a laugh,
But there's a war inside of me.
I battle my identity.
I feel such turmoil and unrest,
I can't shake my anxiety.

This uneasiness and suffering,
Slowly it is draining me.
I'm blank and barren,
I'm lifeless and desolate.
But I can't accept this as my fate.

I hold immense hostility towards myself.
I'm stressed and tense
But in my defense,
This is a learned behavior.

I've taken over the treatment of me,
But I learned it from those who
Said they cared
Then victimized me.

So now I have this riot inside
Between the mistreated me
And the me that knows my worth.
I cannot be defeated by
The me that causes harm.

The victor must be the me that sees the value I possess.
I must find peace, I must find joy,
I must find contentment and love for myself.
Acceptance of myself will be the victory.

This is a constant battle,
It's not one easily won.
It is a conflict I must face
And the destructive me must retreat.
Oh, how this is bittersweet.

For one of me to win, the other me must surrender.
So I'll still lose a part of me.
But I must find prosperity
In knowing I will succeed.

There is a battle within myself
My regard for myself gets stronger.
I aspire and I thrive
On my innermost desires.

This is my own affliction.
I am my own creation.
I build my own foundation.
But I refuse to crumble,
As good triumphs over evil.
Even within myself.

I was finally at a point where I was thinking about my inner peace and happiness, that contentment you only find from within. I started actually seeing the world around me. I started trying to find beauty in all of God's creations. I was, after all, one of them. If He can make the roses, the rainbows, the sunrises and sunsets, seashells, peacocks, sweet little kittens, and so many other fascinating and beautiful fabrications, and He also made me, I have to be pretty special. Oh, what a struggle this was for me. I took so much time being still. Pausing. Seeing the good around me. I really made it harder than it had to be.

<u>Still My Heart Frowns</u>
Staring out the window,
The sun going down,
The outside world so beautiful,
Yet my heart frowns.

Color change of the tree leaves
Snowflakes on the ground
Ocean waves hitting shore
Yet my heart still frowns

Fancy cars passing by
Children playing in the playground
Delicate flowers blowing in the wind
Still my heart frowns

The outside world so beautiful
As the sun goes down
My personal world torn and beaten
In complete darkness
I slowly weaken
As my heart sadly frowns.

The problem was that I couldn't see the beauty because I couldn't see past my own shame and hurt. At this point in my life, I had two children with two different fathers, an ex-husband, and numerous fruitless relationships. I was feeling like I was just making one bad choice after another in my journey to find happiness.

After having my daughter, I realized I could not afford child care for two children on the pay I was receiving. I was barely surviving only paying child care for one, so for the cost to double every month was too much!

It was bad enough I was left covering the housing expenses myself after a failed relationship. It just kept piling on, so I had to make the decision to move back to my hometown in Pennsylvania.

There, I purchased my first home, where my mortgage was only a small fraction of what I was paying in rent in Virginia. And it kind of felt good to call it home. My home. A place where I didn't have to ask permission to paint the walls or change flooring. It was a cute little home with a stream in the backyard. My daughter was just a month old when we moved, but my son was old enough to enjoy this stream and the land. He would go out and catch little minnows and frogs.

My time in this home established my love for real estate as well. I would later go on to become a real estate broker, and it all stemmed from the act of taking a leap of faith, with no real guidance, to purchase this quaint little home.

Moving back to Pennsylvania also allowed me to have help from my mother. She was able to help with child care when I needed it, feed us, and provide emotional comfort that was so much needed for me at this time.

I ultimately fell into a bit of a deep depression in this home, but first, let me give props where it's due. My mother...

<u>My Mother, the Victor</u>
I don't think I have ever given
my mother enough credit throughout life
She worked hard, she sacrificed
She always provided.

She could have left but always stayed,
Worked two jobs, three jobs,
Whatever she had to do
To get the bills paid.

And she did it all on her own with no help
We may not have had everything, but we weren't in need.
We had shelter and food
I hold much gratitude
for the way she raised me.

She had drive all my life, even when she felt hopeless
She never gave up. She held onto a dream
With great hopefulness.
She's a hero, a fighter.

She still isn't where she expected to be in life,
But she's a survivor, determined to lead.
If only she could step outside that rathole town
She may feel what it's like to be free.

Yet she has helped me through some hard times
Within her own limits
Always looked after me through all of my bad decisions
She's an example of good measure,
There is no comparison.

Yes, she makes mistakes, she is human, no doubt.
But I'm thankful she bore me.
She gave me a good life, and I'll carry the torch
So my kids see the victor in her through me.

During this time, I was having a hard time accepting that I was a single mother with two children. I kept dwelling on the mistakes that I'd made in my early adult years. I took some time to just be still, but it kept eating at me that my children were without a father. I wanted so much for them to have a male figure to look up to.

I must say that co-parenting was very important to me with both of their fathers. Unfortunately, my son's father has chosen a life that didn't involve his beautiful being in it. And my daughter's father occasionally participates. But it is important for me to accept and assist in whatever we decide is best for our children. I am here when they need someone to talk to or cry on in regards to their feelings about their fathers, but they will never receive bad information about their fathers from me.

It's important for me to encourage my children and never be a reason they feel a certain way about their father because of anything I have said. I want them to be free to form their own relationships and their own opinions. Children do not choose the life given to them, and they would definitely not choose the life of a fatherless child intentionally...I would never make life harder for them than it has to be. So, when it comes to a relationship with their biological fathers, I am nothing but supportive.

I also feel the urge to note that, while I was embarrassed at some of the situations I put myself through in life, I never ever made my children feel like they had any part of that. They were here for a reason with me. You will never hear me say they were a mistake. They were simply unplanned.

Regardless, I was still lacking that father role model in their life. I tried dating sites and went out with a couple of weirdos, and that never worked out. One guy even took my car and wouldn't bring it back. I had to use a threat to be able to go get it.

One day, I ran into the pastor's son from the church across

the street from my mother's house (I actually think I ran into him there at the church). We have known each other since we were little kids. This was the church where my mother sang the solo when my childhood Christmas got ruined by some thieves. It had been years since I had seen him, and when I ran into him that day, we really hit it off.

I was going through a hard time internally. Since I had my eye on the pastor's son, I decided I wanted to attend the church again after such a long time being away. I didn't just want to spend time with him; I wanted to find out about Jesus. After a couple of visits, however, I heard repeatedly, "If you do this, you will go to hell...if you don't do this, you will end up in hell." I'm sure there were other messages in there, but these types of messages really stood out and stopped me in my tracks. Because of this, I began to acquire a lot of fears and even more self-doubt.

I started questioning every little decision and ultimately every mistake I had ever made. I started dwelling on where I was at that moment in life, and thinking about what would happen if I died that day. I wasn't suicidal or anything, but I had genuine fears about how I was living my life. Would I end up in hell? The way I was living wasn't in alignment with where I wanted to be, and this put me in soul-search mode. Who was I, and who did I want to become?

I was losing self-worth the further I got in this expedition within myself. I wasn't in a good place and started falling fast, especially as it pertained to the pastor's son.

He began cheating on me. He would leave for weeks at a time on drunken beach trips. Many times, his actions showed that he wasn't interested in what I was looking for. Commitment. A family. A father figure for my children.

Don't get me wrong, he was good to my children. And we had some good times. We sang together, and I really enjoyed that. He played the guitar so beautifully, and we harmonized together magically. He also helped me do a lot of work on my house (for which I paid him). He helped me put siding on and finish some of the space inside.

But I definitely gave more to the relationship than I was receiving. He would return, and I would cook, clean, and take care of him when he got sick. I made myself available for him whenever he needed me until the next time he wanted to hang out with other women and his buddies for days and weeks.

I decided that he was toxic and I needed to work on separating from him—not just for myself, but for my children. They deserve the whole world. While my circumstances were not great and I made a lot of mistakes, sometimes over and over, I lived for my children.

Their little eyes were just taking in everything. They were watching what I was permitting and how I allowed him to treat me. They were feeling him leave along with me. Every. Single. Time. They felt disappointment, too. I couldn't allow it to continue. Yes, it was nice having him there, but if he couldn't devote himself to us, then he just wasn't right for us.

Having them gave me a reason to look out for myself. I had to. If I wasn't at my best, how could I care for them 100%? So, in a way, because I was trying to do what was best for them, I was actually doing what was best for me. I avoided a lot of bad situations because my first thought was, *No, my children do not need this in THEIR lives.*

I am definitely not perfect and still made stupid decisions in their young years (and even now that they are older; I am human!). But more often than not, I thought twice before allowing myself to be mistreated. Their little minds were absorbing it all. By providing for them, I ultimately provided for me.

Besides, Psalm 127: 3-5 says, "Children are a gift from God; they are his reward. Children born are like sharp arrows to defend him. Happy is the man who has his quiver full of them. That man shall have the help he needs when faced with his enemies." In fact, this Bible verse is tattooed on my arm to show me that my children are here really to protect me—maybe even to protect me from myself.

At this time, providing meant protecting what they saw and heard. In order to do that, I didn't allow anyone to speak to me in an ill manner. I paid attention to how I was treated, I didn't allow mistreatment, and I set boundaries for myself. I was more aware of what I accepted from others, on full alert to assure they only saw goodness.

I became more in tune with myself and what I would permit. I broke the patterns and addictions that I had throughout my life and stopped allowing different men to come and go. But I had to deal with the existing toxic patterns. The first step was to withdraw and vacate from the relationship with the pastor's son.

In the middle of my break-up with the pastor's son, I left for a two-week drill, and I met Tim, who, at the time, was my instructor for a class I had to take. I was living in Pennsylvania but still drilling in Virginia, so I had to make that drive every month. Otherwise, I would have had to switch to the Pennsylvania National Guard, and I wasn't ready to do that.

Once the class Tim instructed was over, I stayed to help clean the classroom and get to know him better. Afterward, I decided to contact him.

A couple of days after this training, I made a decision to become a surrogate (carry a baby for someone else). I'll share more about my being a surrogate later in this book. All I will say now is that this decision allowed me to be home with my kids. I was trying to break patterns. I was working really hard to end cycles. I was also working hard on turning to myself and loving myself. Yes, my children didn't have their fathers in their lives, but I didn't want a repeat of my childhood where my mother worked all the time. Being a surrogate allowed me to care for my children and raise them, spend time with them, and give them good lives.

I also signed up to go to school. The entire reason I joined the Army was to pay for my college. If I didn't do it at that particular moment, I would have lost the opportunity, and I would have done all of this work for nothing. I have learned through life that I work well under pressure. During what normally took four years, I earned my degree in three years by completing my courses through the summers. And the entire time I was in school, I was also paid from my GI Bill earned through the military. After all, I was still attending monthly weekend drills while my mother helped me with the kids.

I was super-focused on growing as a person and developing my skills. Life was about caring for my children all day, putting them to bed at night, working on schoolwork until 2 a.m., getting up through the night to feed my daughter, who was still a baby, and getting virtually no sleep. Even though each of my kids had a bedroom, I had a daybed in my living room, and that is where we slept every night. In the end, I obtained my bachelor's degree in business management and had accomplished something never done in my immediate family.

Imagine allowing a man to come into my life when I was severing a relationship with a pastor's son, had two children as a single mother, was pregnant with someone else's baby, and was in school full-time. I had no time to sleep, so how was I going to have time to date? What could he possibly think of me?

But Tim didn't judge me and seemed to only want to help make life easier for me. He made me laugh, and at the time, I felt that I needed some laughter in my life. My worry, however, was that I needed some time to be alone...time to pause...time to get to know myself. I needed to spend time with myself without the company of another man. But it didn't happen that way.

I made the first move. For a brief time, I was still somewhat dating the pastor's son, but as that fizzled away, I continued to enjoy any amount of time on the phone I could get with Tim while also enjoying time alone. He was still in Virginia, and I was still living in Pennsylvania. It was nice to have a long-distance relationship where I could have someone to talk to but still focus on me and my kids.

Our first real date was on the Potomac River for the 4th of July. It was beautiful! He took me for a ride on his boat and we saw fireworks on the water. That seems like moons ago, but I remember the hotel we stayed at had a lot of cats around outside. Hahaha...

And I left my cheesecake in the hotel refrigerator when I left. Damnit!

Anyway, I had an amazing time with him. He was a gentleman and treated me so well, but I had such a hard time getting emotionally close to him. I didn't want to rush into anything. What we had was so nice, and I didn't want to ruin it by getting serious. We had fun together, and I feel like since we took our time, got to know each other, and established a friendship first, we went into the relationship with an amazing foundation that took time to build. One brick at a time.

He traveled a lot for work, so in between his trips, he would travel to visit me in Pennsylvania. I didn't make the trip to Virginia often. For a while, I wouldn't get close to him, and I wouldn't allow him to spend time with my children as I had a really hard time with that. But eventually, I let him see that part of me. The better part of me, if I am honest.

This lasted roughly a year, with us telling each other, "we aren't serious." I kept telling myself I was just doing what I do best: getting intimate but not attached. Until I did. I don't even recall when it started getting serious. Small thoughts of him that turned into wanting more and more of him. What a scary feeling to realize I was actually falling in love with him. And my first instinct was to push him away.

<u>Push Away</u>
I realize you feel for me
A love I've never felt before.
I don't deserve your sentiment
And so I deflect, warily...

Apprehensively, I push you away,
I don't know why I do that.
Inside I'm begging you to hold me close,
I don't know how to act.

Every time I try to run,
Every time I say I'm done,
I cry and frown I even pout,
I know you don't even know what it's about.

When I say "go away,"
I'm really pleading on the inside "Oh, please stay!"
What I really mean is "hold me tight,"
Tell me "It will be al 'right."

Understand, it's not your fault.
I'm terrified,
And I don't know how to conduct myself,

It's easier to withdraw
To protect my heart.

Eventually, we got into a rhythm, and I stopped being so dramatic. One day out of the blue, he asked me to move in with him. I think he just did that because he was tired of driving to see me (I'm joking...sort of.). He owned his own home but didn't spend a lot of time there since he traveled so much. Moving in together would allow us to spend slightly more time together.

Of course, I said yes. It was a big step for me, but after a year of dating, we had to advance. I was happy. I felt good. I was in a good space physically, mentally, and emotionally.

I wasn't ready to sell my home, though, so I decided to rent it out. The kids and I made the move to Virginia and worked through some kinks upon arrival. I was so used to not answering to anyone while living on my own. The same was true for him. There were some things we had to have conversations about and ultimately make changes on as we adjusted to a life of living under the same roof. But at the end of the day, life was good.

For a long time, I really struggled with the idea of a man genuinely loving both me and my children. I got in my own way and I pushed him away...a lot. Each time I did, he pulled me in closer and loved me harder, and for that, I will always be grateful. I started to realize I was exactly where I needed to be. My kids were happy. They were provided for. So what if the reason I was finally getting to a point of working on my own happiness was actually for my kids? It was a start!

During one of my surrogacies (maybe the second one?), I started getting irritated that we weren't even engaged yet. Weird, huh? Considering I wasn't looking for anything serious. Ha!

After two solid years of dating, I gave the ultimatum that if I delivered this baby as an unengaged woman, he could start getting boxes because I would be packing my things immediately after.

I went into labor early, and he showed up with a photo of an engagement ring while proposing in the delivery room. It was a photo because he likes to procrastinate and ordered the ring late. That is how he has always been. Procrastinator. He probably ordered the ring on my way to the hospital, but he will never admit that. Of course, I said yes.

Then, we found out I was pregnant not too long after. We weren't planning to have a baby, but we also weren't preventing it. So, at seven months pregnant, we decided to get married. Just our close loved ones came, in a small church, with a small reception after. My mom sang and my brothers were my bridesmaids (haha). It was lovely.

Life was good. He didn't just say "I do" to me that day, he also said it to my children. And afterward, we were both baptized, demonstrating a spiritual meaning to our marriage.

We then went on to have a healthy delivery of our boy, Bernie.

Finally, my kids were not fatherless children! I took time and learned about myself and what it would take to be happy, and I didn't settle for less. I stuck up for myself, and I didn't negotiate in any way. In doing so, I set an example for my children. But it was because of them that I even put any effort into my own happiness and self-love. I grew them in my belly, and I nurtured them from conception throughout every moment of life. After all, they are a part of me, and I am grateful for them. All three of them played a role in my happiness.

I am Them, They are Me

These three amazing beings that shared my body for a time
Tanner, Hana, Bernie...
They are different from the others...they are mine.

Even though I felt too young, I wasn't ready...
The timing wasn't really prime
It turns out I needed them...they saved me...
They are my bloodline.

My legacy will live on through them
Because of that, I must consider how my actions will affect them.
I must always be aware, I must secure their future
I must prepare the way for them.

I must hold regard for the decisions I make
I must act in valor for their sake.
From the day they were born until forevermore.
They are my lineage... the lives of which I bore.

They force me to make better choices
Every minute watching me changes their destiny
It changes their perception of their reality
I am their protector...I am their voice
I am them. They are me.

It is my responsibility
To make their lives good
To raise them. Mold them.
Into and beyond adulthood...

I stand behind them, beside them, in front of them when needed.

I guide them, guard them, comfort them, lead them,
I'd keep them safe forever if I could.

Each of them so different...
One's a little bit country...one is always reading novels...
One won't turn off his game...and as time goes on,
More of their identities unravel.

I'm wrapped around their fingers for eternity.
Even when I'm 80 and they're well into their years...
My purpose on this earth is clear.

They need me. And I need them.
My every move, my every intention...
My every vision, my contemplation...

Stems from their every want and need.
I am committed to a life lived for them.
Yes, I am...yes indeed...
I am them. They are me.

Being with Tim felt different than any other relationship I had ever been in. He always allowed me to be me. He allowed me to make decisions for myself and even work on myself. And, ohhh, does he make me laugh.

I really need that.

Every single day of my life, I am happy and laughing. My advice to my children is now—always look for people that make you laugh. It is so important! I do give Tim some credit, but I also acknowledge that I took the time to get to know myself and what I like and don't like, and this has made all of the difference in where I am right now.

Up until this point, I was so eager to make others happy that I disregarded my own happiness. And I'm not sure if I would have ever regarded my own happiness if it weren't for making the move to Virginia with Tim. I don't know if I would have had the means to do so. Life somehow got easier.

Yes, some of it had to do with the fact that I wasn't struggling financially like I had my entire life up until this point. I was learning about a credit score and how to budget and save. That was huge because that allowed me to not constantly live in survival mode but to have the will to explore myself a little. After all, he handled the majority of the bills, and that gave me the time and ability to figure out my employment wants so that I could work on being self-sufficient.

Even though I wasn't struggling, I still had some serious issues to work through as an adult because of what I went through in my early years. Because I have lived poor, and after my separation, even spending some time in a hospital, in jail, and being homeless, I have a hard time with money hoarding sometimes. It is a constant struggle to get through. I just have a hard time letting money go! This means I sometimes pay bills late because I am afraid to empty my bank account. Then, there are consequences for doing so, like late payment fees. I am still a work in progress and always learning. Tim was always hearing me cry about overdraft fees in the early months of us living together.

In the middle of all of this, the tenant of my very first home in Pennsylvania decided to move out. I used this as the perfect opportunity, and I sold my home. Not only had we earned rent off of the home, but we also ended up selling it for double what I paid for it.

At this point, I relied on myself and turned to myself more. I put extensive work into myself, and I spent time exploring what made me happy. I started caring for myself. I really started finding time for myself, especially when Tim traveled for periods of time for work. I love being alone...and it turns out my husband is the best person to be alone with.

With You

You are my peace,
My sanity.
You've never given up on me.

You lead me into normalcy,
With your clear mind and spirited heart,
You bring my life stability.

You are playful and witty
And charming and lively,
And batty and funny.

By being the best you,
You bring out the best in me.
Happiness consumes me
When I am with you.

You make sure I'm healthy
And you genuinely care for me.
You work so hard as you provide
Our family with security.
You fulfill all of our needs.
I have no doubts or worries
When I am with you.

There is power in your silence

Authority in your softness.
Vitality in your calmness.
Comfort in your smile.

I'm living in paradise...
Happiness is enjoying life with you.

Tim travels a lot—however, even though my past has shown that I react when I feel abandoned, I never felt abandoned with his work needs. And ironically, he works at the place my ex-husband went to work. The difference is, Tim comes home every night that he isn't traveling all over the world.

I don't remember when I wrote this, but it was clearly on Valentine's Day while he was traveling for work.

My Valentine Boo
Another year, you are away...
And I can't look you in the eyes and say
The things I'd like to say to you
My Valentine, my heartbeat, my boo...

What I want to say is:

My entire life I've hungered for YOU
You're rare, distinct, unparalleled, unique
There's no one else on earth like you...
My Valentine, my flame, my boo.

When you are here or when you're away,
internally content in absolute peace
In so many ways I escape in you
My desire, my treasure, my boo.

Hour by hour, day by day, it goes too fast when I'm with you
Decelerate the hands of time just a little please
I find my existence in my moments with you,
My Valentine, my affection, my boo.

In a chaotic world you are my calm, my stillness
my pause, my happy place—whether here or away...
In the silence, in total subdue, I find myself in you.
My eternity, my order, my boo.

You are my comfortable paradise
You satisfy my every breath
You provide for me in so many ways
My physical flesh, my spiritual being
You understand my needs, my feelings

And for all of these reasons and so many more
In a wordless chant or a deafening quiver
I exclaim to the world all the days that I roam
I...love...you...and I'm heartsick when you are gone...
My knight, my kingdom, my boo.

Tim fits me in ways I couldn't have imagined. Where I am weak, he has strength and vice versa. For instance, I HATE to cook. But Tim cooks so well...and I love to eat! He likes to be outdoors, and I flourish inside. So he handles the yard and outside upkeep, and I handle the inside. He likes to take the boys fishing and hunting and plays sports outside, and I like to do the inside fun like crafts and game nights. I am soft, and he is an authority. We work very well together.

Once I started getting to know myself and what I liked and didn't like, what made me happy and what made me sad, where I wanted to be in life, who I enjoyed time with and who I didn't, what I liked to do and what I didn't like to do...life was starting to make sense to me. For the first time, maybe ever, I was happy. And while I had help along the way, I made the effort to show up for myself every single day.

Self-Reflection:

1. Do you have certain people in your life who help you work on yourself? When I say "turn to self," it is okay to have others around you helping you while you work on yourself. Just make sure you are relying on yourself, doing for yourself and ultimately finding yourself. For me, I had different times in my life when different people played a role in supporting me so I could work on myself. I found myself most when I was alone. But I also found support when my mother helped me emotionally or when Tim provided a stable place for me to figure myself out. Who can you turn to when you need to work on yourself?

____

____

____

____

____

2. Are there certain people who make you feel less worthy? Eliminate them from your life. I know this is easier said than done, but find ways in which you can remove these toxic people from your life. For instance, I knew the pastor's son was no good for me, so I literally left the state for two weeks for my Army annual training and met Tim. And I know it doesn't make sense, but it was good for me that he didn't live near me. It was safe for me to not be able to just do what I did and run to intimacy. Sometimes, it takes finding another job or losing a number to completely eliminate a person who is toxic from your life.

____

____

____

____

____

____

3. Are there events that have happened that may have taken away from your self-worth? How did you get through these events? Use your inner powers and get committed to your own happiness and awareness. For me, I find power in making lists for myself. You wouldn't believe it if you knew me because I am not super organized or anything. I just find energy in writing things down for me to continue to look back on. Lists of what makes me happy. Lists of what I need to do to get through something. I make lists for everything! What are some ways you can demonstrate commitment to yourself when feeling like an event has overtaken you?

4. What are some ways you restore the value you place on yourself? We have all gone to a dark place at some point in our lives. How do we not only get through it but flourish and maybe even grow because of it? I am big on not only choosing a word of the year for myself (in 2021, my word was "alignment," and I made sure everything I did, every person I met, every word I spoke, every place I went, was in alignment with the goals I set. And now in 2022, my word is "simplify." I am purposely removing things or adding things that simplify my life).

I am also big on setting goals and looking at them often. These goals are a pledge to myself that I am going to spend every chance I get on bettering myself, even when I don't always feel like it. I time block and do other success actions to assure I am always moving forward and never moving backward. Create your own goals and choose a word of the year that you can look at on occasion to remind you of what you want for yourself.

5 Use this as a guide for your word and goals:

WORD OF THE YEAR: To choose your word of the year, create a list (here we go again!) of words that mean something to you as being powerful in that moment. Reflect on the words that came to mind, and choose the one that resonates most with where you wish to be in the near future. Live this word every chance you can.

____

____

____

____

____

Where would you like to be in five to ten years (think about job, money, travel, cars, relationships, your home and where you live, spirituality, education, personal and professional growth, development, etc.)?

____

____

____

____

____

What about one year? Six months? This month? Next week? Today? Write it all down.

____

____

____

____

____

How much money do you need to survive? How much money do you need to live comfortably? How much money do you need to serve your community and give to causes that matter to you?

____

____

____

____

____

How much time do you want for yourself? How much time will you need to be able to effectively serve others?

____

____

____

What causes mean the most to you? Do you wish you could end child hunger? Homelessness? Save all the animals? If you didn't have to work and had all the money you could imagine, where would you spend your time and financial efforts to make a difference in this world?

____

____

____

____

____

What do you need to do to get this amount of money? For me, I sell real estate, so it is easy to assess how many homes I need to sell. Whatever your profession is, what kind of professional goal can you set for yourself to achieve these numbers?

____

____

____

____

____

Who in your life can help you get there?

____

____

____

____

____

Make sure this life you are living and these goals you are setting for yourself are for YOU and not anyone else. Refer to these goals and your word of the year often. Create this plan for yourself, and make sure your short-term goals are stepping stones to meet your long-term goals. With every step you take, you are focusing on how you can make your life better for YOU, whether it is in health, love, finance, business, happiness, spirituality, or any other goals you set for yourself.

This chapter is about turning to myself. In turning to myself, I focused on my mental, emotional, spiritual and physical needs. And as a part of meeting these needs for myself, I had to have a starting point. I had to figure myself out and I had to get to know myself. Since I am a list maker, I had to begin focusing on my goals and what I wanted out of life. So that's what I did, and you should too!

Now, let's go out there and kick ass while checking things off of our lists and meeting the goals we set for ourselves!! Don't look for a knight. Find that sword and handle your own damn business.

chapter 4

LIST OF WAYS I FIND HAPPINESS

As you have probably seen by now, I like to make lists, and I like to put stuff in writing. There is energy in writing things down. I love the fire I feel when I write, and that fire is rekindled every time I read my writing again and again. So here's my list of things that make me happy. While going through it, begin to think of things that make you happy so you can prepare your own list.

1. Say "fuck"...a lot. It's magical and versatile. I love it. And when others say it, it makes me smile.
2. Laugh...a lot.
3. Cry if you need to. Let it out. Just don't stay there.
4. If marriage is your thing, marry someone who makes you laugh every day. Our spouses really are our better halves.
5. Surround yourself with people who make you happy, and eliminate people who don't.
6. Spend some time alone. It really is good for the soul.
7. Connect with people. Join groups.
8. Listen to music.
9. Sing.

10. Dance.

11. Play an instrument.

12. Play a game.

13. Crochet or do a craft.

14. Write. (As you know by now, I enjoy writing poetry.)

15. Tell a story.

16. Call a good friend.

17. Read a good book.

18. Watch a movie.

19. Go shopping.

20. Grow a garden.

21. Drink coffee or tea.

22. Dress up.

23. Dress down/be a bum and make comfortability a priority.

24. I love color, so I always try to be colorful! I wear crazy colors, colorful makeup, I color my hair (it is hot pink right now)...

25. Get tattoos. I like to put my story on my body.

26. Have cheesecake for breakfast.

27. Sleep or rest. Be still.

28. Stay busy.

29. Rearrange furniture.

30. Have someone clean your home.

31. Stay in the house and make your home your place of comfort.

32. Get out of the house/travel the world.

33. Speak your mind, and don't hold anything in.

34. Control your tongue and think before you speak.

35. Get a pet. I chose two hairless cats, a Lykoi (werewolf cat), a hairless dog, and a Bedlington terrier; they complete our family.

36. Have children. They are amazing and make every moment special. (Note: This is my list of things that make me happy. Obviously this isn't for everyone. But I do think creating a family is important. This looks different for everyone, and sometimes it

doesn't even involve blood relatives. I just acknowledge here that for me, happiness was found in having my children).

37. Learn, and never stop learning.

38. Find a career that you enjoy.

39. Wake up and wash daily. Bathing rejuvenates and refreshes you. It helps avoid diseases and builds immunity.

40. Eat right. Let the food and nourishment you take in be your medicine. Heal yourself from the inside, and keep toxicities out of your body.

41. Fast if your body needs to start over and correct itself.

42. Meditate.

43. Use crystals and their healing power to bring out the energy you need.

44. Light a candle or diffuser. Aromatherapy is magic.

45. Turn on mood lights for an added way to change your mood.

46. Diet if needed.

47. Exercise, go for a walk, do yoga, move your body.

48. Get to know your body and what feels good and doesn't feel good.

49. Have sex. Yes, even though it has been used as a coping method in the past for me, if done in a healthy way, it can really get you in tune with yourself and your partner.

50. Drink water.

51. Get outside with nature. Get fresh air and sunshine.

52. Bring nature in, including flowers and plants. I personally do not like cut flowers. I feel like the most beautiful ones are picked just to die to then cease being what I love. I'd rather be surrounded by potted flowers and plants.

53. Color. I have an adult book of cuss words to color.

54. Go to church.

55. Go Geocaching. I use an app found at www.geocaching.com. Life is a treasurehunt!

56. Help others/make others happy/Pay it forward (see list in Chapter 7).

This is my list! What's yours? If you feel up to it, I would love to hear your list. You can send it to commahappyenjoythepause@gmail.com. I'm sure I have missed some and would love to feel inspired to add to my list.

Writing lists provides structure for me. It organizes my thoughts and needs onto paper to see and read out loud. It also provides a guide for me to turn to when I need ideas. It gives me a plan to follow and a physical presence that I can check off as I do the items on the list. Furthermore, it provides satisfaction as I am able to complete items from the list. It also helps me remember things. As we know, I am very forgetful.

This list in particular allows me to feel the accomplishment every time I choose to do an item. Writing lists clears my mind and allows me to think about the tasks at hand. It allows me to put my energy into the right things and not put effort into things that don't serve me in that moment. In addition, it provides focus and drive for me. Maybe it is my way to bring order to my mind, which is sometimes filled with chaos.

I find it odd that I even thrive in list-making, to be honest. After all, I am left-handed, which means I am right-brained. I am mainly impulsive; this much is true. So maybe writing lists makes me feel more in control of myself and my thoughts. Either way, I flourish more when I have a list in my hand.

Each day, you will wake up with different wants, different needs, and different feelings. That's why there are some things on this list that contradict each other, like dressing up and dressing down, going to church and saying fuck a lot, speaking your mind and controlling your tongue. Obviously, you may not be able to do both things at the same time. Just do what fits you for that moment.

Self-Reflection:

1. Make your own list of things that make you happy. A blank page has been provided for you. And feel free to add more pages if needed. The longer the list, the more you have to choose from each day.

____

____

____

____

____

____

2. Make it a goal to do at least one thing from this list. Every. Single. Day. This is a part of self-care and is vital to a happy life.

____

____

____

____

____

____

active self-labor

chapter 5

THOU SHALT FIND YOUR GOALS AND PASSIONS TO FULFILL YOUR PURPOSE

I'm going to be honest and tell you that I really struggled with finding what the hell I was on this earth for. I've always been a free spirit, and I never even thought about my calling until later into my adult years. I feel like I spent a lot of my life in survival mode. How could I help someone else when I didn't have my shit together myself?

I never had the opportunity to think about my future because I could never get out of the past and present. I was stuck during a lot of my life and didn't really have a mentor to teach me about planning for my future. My mother was the only adult figure I could count on, and while she was a hard worker, she was also in a rut a lot of her life. I think she still is. She is still in the same shit town doing the same shit type of work and living the same shit life. I've tried over the years to bring her to Virginia with me, but something is keeping her there. Maybe she has something there that she enjoys. Maybe she feels her purpose is to make a difference there. I am not sure. All I know is that I wasn't living there. I was just existing. Leaving that town was my opportunity to grow and learn about life and myself, gain experience, and maybe even gain some wisdom along the way.

I can't pinpoint a specific person who taught me about planning my life, creating goals, or finding my passions and using them for the better good of the world. I think it was inside me all along. I just had to find a moment in my life where I could be still long enough to breathe and figure it all out.

I have always had a giving and serving heart. I always knew that I was going to do big things. Maybe not on a large scale, but I always had a gut feeling, especially in the midst of turmoil, that I was going through hard times in order to help someone else through the same thing. I genuinely feel that we all struggle and go through hard times for the sole purpose of being able to help the next person.

Once I got to a point in life where I could catch my breath, where I was becoming more stable, where I could learn about myself and what I wanted and needed out of life, I started reading a lot of books. I started watching the habits of successful people and trying to get to a place where I could mimic their actions. I even started watching my husband. After all, I never really felt stability until I was feeling HIS stability. Even though his goals and passions are different from mine, he is secure and made me feel free to explore the same lifestyle. He is balanced and consistent, protective and secure, sane, sound, and trustworthy, happy and established. He is responsible and has a profound permanence to his existence. And he is in a position where he can give freely and help others when they are in need. I desperately wanted that! He had all of the qualities I was looking for, so it only made sense to watch him.

Of course, I wasn't in the same place in life that my husband was. He had the same job since he was seventeen years old. He has built a stable life for himself. He has a good schedule and the means to live out his passions. He is a good ol' country boy who enjoys time outdoors, hunting, fishing, and living the life. And I was on a mission to find the same thing. I wanted freedom of time and craved the means to dig into myself, learn what made me happy, and fulfill that happiness in my own way.

This started by being in tune with my goals in life. I had to really imagine what I wanted life to look like and figure out what I needed to do to get there. This involved coming up with some immediate goals, short-term goals, and long-term goals. Turn back to Chapter 3 to dig inside of yourself to find what you want out of life. Where do you see yourself, and how can you get there? Where does your passion lie? What grabs at your heart? We are all put here for a reason. We are sewn and woven into who we are with purpose in mind, and every molecule in our being swirls around in a life web that reflects our purpose. This includes our passions, our likes, and our dislikes. It is all intertwined.

At the same time that I was figuring myself out—my wants, needs, goals, and passions—I was writing my list above in Chapter 4 of the things I have found that make me happy. This list has been so helpful in molding me on the inside. I hope to add to this until the day I die. I love exploring myself and finding new things that spark feelings and life within me. And one of my goals will always be to try to do at least one thing from this list every single day.

When it comes down to writing my goals, the truth is that these goals have changed over and over again throughout my life, so I am no expert in figuring this out for someone else. When I write my objectives, typically at the beginning of each year, I will start with immediate goals, then short- and long-term goals. A lot of the time, I have intentions of bringing all of these goals to fruition, but once I get going into my immediate goals, I some-times have to adjust and alter my short- and long-term targets.

In the end, it always turns out the way it should be, but sometimes my goals don't align with reality. Sometimes, what I want to do or where I want to be must be put off or happens earlier than I thought it would. Putting things in writing isn't the be-all and end-all. It is just putting energy into motion. When we write things down, it creates this vibe within us that sets us into action mode.

I always start with my passion. This is the baseline of the goals I create and the purpose I set for myself. When I start with my passions, I rarely end up doing things or getting into an employed position that I don't enjoy. I am firm that if it isn't fun, it isn't for me. From the time I got past struggle and had the means to start working on and within myself, every move I made in life had purpose and was done with intention. It's always pleasing and gratifying for me when making these moves, no matter how big or small my moves are. I am not saying I have enjoyed everything that I have ever done or every job I have ever had in life. But if it was something I didn't particularly enjoy, it was just a stepping stone to get me to where I wanted to be.

I have always had a drive to work hard and a determination to be somebody, but from the start, I was working to live, not flourish. I got my first job when I was eleven. I had a paper route in my neighborhood from age eleven until I left for boot camp at eighteen. Yes, this job got my foot in the door to gaining experience in the work field, and it required me to get up very early every single day, but I met some amazing people doing this. I would sit and talk to some of the elders of the neighborhood as I delivered their papers to them. They rewarded me with good tips on holidays. And I began learning about work ethic and earning my money through working hard. Even though I didn't know the term at eleven years old, customer satisfaction was very important to me. I didn't want to disappoint those waiting on their daily paper. Sometimes it was hard, like when the big dogs would jump at me or when it was storming, but this experience set the path for how I would perform in positions to come.

At twelve, I started babysitting and continued that throughout my life. I really enjoyed caring for other people's children. Even though some would argue that I was just a child myself, and I just might even agree with them, there was satisfaction in earning money to play, eat, go on walks, and do things I was doing anyway. After all, I was also doing these things for my brother, too. What's a couple more to join the party?

And at sixteen, I got a job at the arcade in the mall until I left for the Army at age eighteen. Who wouldn't want to get paid to play video games? Okay, so I wasn't supposed to be playing, but when there wasn't anyone else in there, what else would I have done besides catching up on homework?

I've always worked, and I really plan on working until the day I die, whether I get paid for it or not. We spend a lot of our waking time at work, so I think, ultimately, employment ends up taking a big portion of our goal-setting. How much do we need to make? Where would we like to work? How many hours a day do we want to spend earning a living, and how many hours of free time do we wish to have? These are very important questions when it comes time to sit down and plan our ideals.

From the age eighteen, once I completed Army training, I found employment in many different areas that were all rewarding in some way or another. I've worked with people with intellectual/developmental disabilities. Of course, this was rewarding as I had experience and could relate through helping my brother throughout life. I say that lightly because the reality is, he helped me throughout life, too. My brother has an intellectual disability, but you can't tell him that! An IQ number means nothing to him.

I've worked at a yogurt shop, a car wash company and a carport sales company. I've worked doing supply admin at Fort Lee. And each of these positions led me to the next best thing and the next opportunity. Yes, there were times when I took a job because it fulfilled my needs of providing food and shelter, but those positions usually didn't last long. They were, however, stepping stones to where I am today. They gave me knowledge and experience to prepare me for what was to come next. I learned how to work with people. I learned about teamwork and working alone to get tasks done. I learned how to put the customer first, how to consider accuracy when giving change back to the customer, about sales numbers, and about making top dollar while still making sure prices were fair.

During some times in my life, I changed jobs a lot because I didn't get along with management or I moved on to a better paying job. With each change I made, I gained more of an understanding and added to my resume, building a background in different positions.

Sometimes, life experiences mold our passions for us. For instance, I have a heart for children who are fatherless. I also have a heart for women who feel their self-worth is in having a man. I feel for those suffering from addiction. I've been in these situations. I also feel passionate about helping those with disabilities because of my brother.

Maybe you have found some things that you are particularly good at. I found that I am really good at crocheting. I make sure I use that talent to help others. I crochet scarves, hats, blankets, and other things for the homeless, and I whip up designs for my children when they ask for them. Along with that, I also enjoy design. I am trying to figure out how that fits into my life at the moment, but I know it relates to my real estate business. Every day, I think about what I enjoy, and I try to do more of that. Your passions don't have to be used for income, though. Sometimes, your passions are simply there just to fulfill a void in your life. Sometimes, we connect with a movement, or event, or activity, or scenario just because it is a part of us. And it's okay to never use it to make a living.

But if you want to use your passions for income, will you need specific training to get there? I joined the Army not only to work on myself and my inner struggles but also to better myself by going to college without debt. They paid for my entire four-year degree. I didn't earn my degree until ten years after I joined the Army, but I did it! I earned my bachelor of science in business management from Liberty University. I did it all online, as that was all I could commit to at that moment. And maybe that's how it was intended to be because college was not even conducted online back when I joined the Army.

Once I earned my degree, however, I realized that there wasn't much I could do with it. But in the whole scheme of things, I did learn about managing a business and starting my own business. So in that sense, it was the perfect degree to get into with the free spirit that I am. I may one day go back to school just because I love learning, but two years after I earned my degree, after bouncing from job to job, I decided I wanted to sell real estate.

As you recall, my love for real estate started when I bought my first home in Pennsylvania. During my time in this home, I worked hard to improve it. I replaced the siding, I added square footage by finishing some space in the attic and basement, and I painted and replaced the flooring. It was cozy living there, and when I moved out, I made money off of renting it out and then ultimately sold it for double what I had paid for it. I knew then that real estate was a good, flexible way to earn income around other things I had going on in my life.

A couple years went by, and I didn't quite know I would make somewhat of a living off of real estate until my husband and I decided to start looking for our first home together. When I left Pennsylvania and moved in with him, I was moving into HIS home that he built before we met. For some reason, I had a hard time living there. Maybe it was the culture shock—I was used to living in the city, so moving to twenty-five acres was tough on me. Or maybe it was how close we lived to his family and the fact that I didn't have that kind of support. Maybe it was that a family member of his and I butted heads.

Whatever the reason, when we were ready to find our first home together, the experience was so exciting and extraordinary for me! I know we drove our real estate agent crazy with all of the homes I wanted to get into and look at. It was thrilling and adventurous. And I just knew I wanted to have access to houses available for purchase. I wanted to be notified first as homes hit the market.

We were very strategic as we got into the real estate world. Over the years, we have used Tim's VA loan, and I have used my VA loan benefits when needed, too. We would typically buy homes that had a second family dwelling that we could manage easily. We would rent out the apartment or second home on the property, and it would pay for most of our mortgage. We would follow the tax law and live in it two out of the last five years and then sell so we didn't get a huge tax hit.

Relaxing, to me, was sitting down at the end of the day and turning on a home decorating show or flipping through a home design magazine. I have always enjoyed getting deep into a good home project or doing something to add value to my home. I'm sure my husband didn't know what he was signing up for when he met me, and I have had a long to-do list of home project needs ever since (haha). And even when I am content with where I am in life, I am still always scouring real estate opportunities that I may or may not be able to afford.

A girl can dream!

I love the flexibility that comes with working for myself, which is much-needed being married to a man who is gone a lot with his work. He is on active duty with the Army and typically travels roughly two weeks out of every month. During these times when I am at home with the kids, I carry the responsibilities we would both share.

I love the freedom and the ability to do different things with my real estate license. I can work as much or as little as I want to. Some years, I work part-time. Some years, I work full-time helping others sell their homes and find their next stepping stone or permanent home. Some years, I only refer business to other agents and earn money on that, too, while still having my hand in the process. A few years ago, I earned my broker license because it allows me even more freedom in that I can open my own brokerage one day. I can also hold my real estate license in multiple locations, whereas with a sales license, I am confined to just holding it in one brokerage at a time.

At this very moment, I am an associate broker with Sentry Residential, and I am the principal broker for Estately and HWE Virginia. At Sentry, most of our agents are either military spouses or veterans, so being here allows me to connect with the people I am destined to help. At Estately, they have a business model that brings in homes from the MLS (multiple listing services, which is the database for listing agents to list properties for sale, and selling agents to share properties with their buyer clients), and they use my license to do so. My role with HWE is similar, except it is commercial. I don't have a leadership role per se, but this structure allows me to have classes and licenses paid for by them. Step by step, I am molding my real estate career into what I need it to be at this moment.

I also have a goal of one day starting a nonprofit. I'd like to purchase land for cheap and build tiny houses or affordable housing on it in order to help people who are struggling to find housing. I push to stop homelessness, addiction, domestic violence, and assist foster kids who age out and have nowhere to go. My hope is to build a space where we can help people build credit, help others with jobs, career classes and workshops, and help homeownership dreams come true. The good ol' American Dream!

When you are following your passions, you are really paving a way to an amazing, exciting life. Your journey will make sense when you uncover the things you care so much about that you are willing to suffer to achieve it (the Latin word "*Pati*" means to suffer and helped form the word "passion"). Suffering isn't always a bad thing. There is growth in suffering. The ability to help others by actually putting yourself in their shoes opens the way to ministry opportunities. After all, God uses our hands and feet. We are all connected. When someone is in need, those around them will chip in and take care of that need in a way that only God can orchestrate.

Ever see someone in need and think to yourself, *What can I do to help them?* Or ever have a friend go through something you went through and then have the ability to relate and comfort? Or maybe you earned extra on your paycheck this week and had just enough to help your neighbor who was about to lose her home? Sometimes, we hear a message and just know we heard that in order to share it with someone else it relates to. I am a firm believer that when we hear a voice or get a tug to help someone, that is God.

And when I get that tug, I don't have to be asked twice. I

jump right up and do it. I rarely regret it either. Even if I give to someone who has ill intentions with what I am giving, that is for them to work through. That burden doesn't fall on me. I have taken long pauses in my life, but the second I get that calling, I am on it. I am a bit impulsive at times. I am not sure if that is really me or God, but it doesn't matter. Everything happens in God's time because He knows me, and He knows my heart already. He knows He only has to ask me once.

He uses human channels to get things done in earthly form. I am simply a vessel while here on this earth.

It took me a long time to realize that Jesus lives inside of us, inside of me and therefore it is up to me to fulfill my needs. I know this sounds so bizarre that my friends' hands and feet are helping me because they are acting in an already arranged series of events that their mind has no recollection of, but still they reach out to me, offer me a listening ear, or a helping hand at just the right time. This predetermined destiny can only be God. That's all I know.

Throughout my life, I don't know how else to explain it other than to say that I had divine help. When I was in need, someone was always sent to me. When I had pennies, a check came in the mail or I found a hundred dollar bill in the parking lot. A stranger from a new church brought me groceries to fill my bare refrigerator. I found a kitten when I needed to feel loved. Something always happened, and someone always entered my life right when I needed it. Quite supernatural, really.

All of these vessels were brought into my life. And I am also a vessel because Jesus is in me. And Isaiah 6:1 says "...I saw the Lord high and exalted, seated on a throne, and the train of His robe filled the temple." Can you imagine? He is soooo big that just the hem of His coat fills the temple!! In those days, the longer the train of the robe, the more powerful and victorious the king wearing it was, as they would cut off the train of a defeated king and add it to their train of victory. Therefore, the enemy is already defeated. Let's start living our lives as such.

Perhaps this Bible verse means that, in getting just the hem into the temple, we are speaking of our bodies as the temple, and each of us has just a piece of how big the Higher Being really is as it pertains to being inside of us.

After all, WE ARE THE TEMPLE (1 Cor 3:16 says, "Don't you know that you yourselves are God's Temple and that God's Spirit dwells in your midst?")—our spirits, our minds, our souls, the depth of our beings are the roots of where our emotions come from, channeled towards helping others, and Jesus is so involved within us that just the train of His robe fills our temple. Crazy, right? We are bound to do big things for others!

<u>Purpose</u>

If you're not building, you're crumbling.
I struggled so long, surviving, not thriving.
I know there's a reason for my existence
Even when I was in no condition
To be a blessing in every moment to every person.

How can I help someone through their mess?
When I was just going through the motions
I was in my own distress
Drowning in oceans of all of my tears...

What was the meaning of my creation?
—I didn't know—

Until I spent time building my foundation
I needed to get grounded

Stop resisting, stop hesitating
I'm destined for rewarding contribution
if only I would allow it.

My headquarter, my home base is
Inside of me and has been all along.
My spirit is free, wild, and untamed
Unless it has to be.

I can be civilized in necessity
As long as I'm woven in the depths of good merit
To be of value and benefit,
Useful for the goodwill of mankind.

That is my purpose
To love and accept, declare my respect
To the reckless prodigal—
I am drawn to the masses left shunned by the world,
Those unlovable to the public eye,
The outcasts, the homeless, the foreign, the forsaken,
The sentenced, rejected, unwanted, forgotten.

Society is throwing stones at them,
All the while I'm gathering them to build them up.
Each and every abandoned soul
Loving them to new heights.

Building empires and skyscrapers,
Constructing essence into their being.
Firm foundation, solid ground.
Substantial vessels will never sink in quicksand.

I was the outcast throughout some of my life,
And some took chances on me. Building my foundation
Brick by brick, stone by stone, building me up,
And as I rose, I was determined to take others with me.
The very nature of community.

New opportunity to see the world from a higher view.
Even in the midst of what I was going through,
I could see the difference others were making in me
And knew I could do the same.
There's growth in suffering.
As long as you always go back home.

And soon, when you make it over the horizon,
You will see your life experiences
Were meant to occur
So you could rise up and all could see
There's hope in you...

From ocean shore to ocean shore,
Human channeling,
Rivers of accomplishments,
The veins of life throughout the world.

My divine love for humanity
and those with the same purpose as me
Has continued this infrastructure of humankind.
Our home's house love, it radiates. Draws the next person in.

Til I wander to the next destination,
I live life fully, spreading love across the cosmos.
In tune with the roads and waterways,

I travel far, and then I plant myself,
If only for a moment, until my next terminal
My next landing place...

Coming full circle over and over again
Building regions around the land.
Hinged on love in different phases.
As the world rotates as it was always designed to,
We are all connected in our purpose.

One leading to the next
Until we are all developed and erect
Each man and beast a work in progress...
Each living soul, designed by the great Architect.
And a crumbling world is not in His masterplan.

When we open ourselves to give, we open ourselves to also receive. I think we receive so that we can give, and when we give, we receive more abundantly. Letting our passion bleed into our goals leads to a great mix of contentment in every facet of life and gives us the opportunity to live more fully. Your passions and goals can change throughout your lifetime; as your life changes, your wants and needs change, and maybe even the needs of those around you change.

I choose to live by the spirit through the concept of love. I'm no longer bound by fear as I once was so long ago. By living in the spirit of love, I love everyone and genuinely care about humanity. I aim to do good and be good. God has put you on earth—right here, right now—for a reason. This moment in time was meant to encapsulate your life in it. You were born for such a time as this! Use this time to be living proof of God. We all have a purpose. Proverbs 16:4 says, "The Lord has made everything for its purpose, even the wicked for a day of disaster." Even the bad things that happen to us have purpose. That is kinda hard to wrap my brain around. But without the bad, we couldn't see goodness. During this spiritual battle of good versus evil, you were needed in this time and space on earth.

You.

My struggle is that I want to do so much and life is so short. I want to save every human and animal. I want to travel the world. I want to read every book and learn everything there is to know. I want to hear everyone's story and cram everything I possibly can into this short life I have been given.

My purpose is different from my goals and passions that we talked about earlier. My passions may have led to my purpose, and my goals may have helped me get there, but I have learned that a lot of my self-contentment came with finding my purpose. And I genuinely believe that a part of my purpose is just to love and accept.

Considering that I struggle with closeness and don't like to be touched, this may sound strange. I see myself as being hard to love, but at the same time, I have a divine love for humanity that I just can't explain in words. Maybe it's because I've been judged. I understand what it feels like to feel unhappy and unloved. I've been the outcast. At the same time, I do believe if Jesus were here, He would hang out with me. Jesus had a way of dining with the sinner and walking with the wanderer.

I'm passionate about equality for all, especially for those in society who have been forsaken. Everyone deserves the right to happiness. Whether they live how you think they should or not. Periodt.

Throughout my life, I've learned that I'm full of love and acceptance, especially for those deemed unlovable in the public eye. I am drawn to those the world has shunned. The hate heaved at them is designed to destroy and tear them down. I use love to build and heighten new life, new hope and new opportunity in them.

Once love is the basis of those once deemed rejected and unworthy, the entire construction of their foundation and the structure being built inside and around them will not fall. Their homes can then house love to help the next person. See, even my analogies correspond to my passions (real estate). HA!

At the end of the day, my life passion lies in loving and accepting all while trying to bridge a gap in society against those who have been deserted and abandoned in the public eye. Of course, I do struggle with my purpose sometimes. And occasionally, I have to think small and assess my relevance for the day instead of thinking about the broader picture of my existence. Some days, my purpose is just to spread love and positive light. Some days, my purpose is to bring love to others, like by bearing others a child. At times, I bear a lot of weight on my shoulders, and I am at the right place at the right time to talk someone off a ledge so to speak. And some days, I recognize that I am human, and I just lay low so I don't cause a feeling opposite of love.

HA!

But I am very in tune with what I need to do day by day to get to my next stepping stone or to meet someone in the middle of their journey.

For someone who spent time in the military, I sure do not like being told what to do! And I had an issue with the brokerage where I began my real estate career.

I did very well my first year in real estate. I won a "Rising Star" award for my production and really enjoyed learning there. That was until I was getting ready to sign up for Homes for Heroes, a nonprofit that works with connecting people who serve with lenders and real estate agents and other professionals who will give back a portion of our commission at closing. I was told I couldn't because they were not a "discount brokerage." I'm not exactly sure what they meant by this. I guess they thought the public would perceive them as giving discounts based on the actions of the salespeople. It didn't make sense to me because they weren't giving a discount at all. The discount was coming out of MY pay. And to me, it wasn't a discount in any sense. It was giving back to those who give so much to all.

This made me feel a certain way. So I then spent a couple of years trying out different brokerages. I never connected to any of them. Some had higher expectations than I was willing to put forth, like requiring a certain sales number or certain hours worked per week. Some required a ton of training time or working from the office. But after much time, I finally really connected with my current brokerage. As I mentioned earlier, I am now a part of a brokerage where a large percentage of the agents are either veterans, military spouses, or somehow connected to the military. I just had to pause, research, and let the right opportunity come to me. I am now in control of how I want to give back, and it is so freeing.

I have this carefree, wild spirit that has a hard time settling on any one thing. I can't believe I have held my real estate license for so long! Ten years is a big deal for me! I think I've been able to do so because no two days in real estate are alike. I can change and alter my business in many different directions all under my real estate broker license. I can still be creative. I don't have defined rules to follow other than treating people fairly and following a structure of organization and bylaws. Other than that, I am learning and growing every day, and each day is a new adventure!

Just for a tidbit of why I love what I do, I wrote this poem for my most recent client, who lost her husband and was selling her home that she lived in for her entire marriage and life with him. Oh, how meaningful and heartfelt it is for me to serve my clients in all of their life challenges and celebrations!

The Walkway of Flowers

You've walked past these flowers,
For years, never a thought
That one day it may be the last.
They've led you to your home of love,
Your walkway to serenity
If only you could go back to that.

But now you are in a new place
With only memories to live by.
But oh, how joy embraces you
When graced with a flashback.

If you could turn back time,
I'm sure you wouldn't change a thing.
Most never get to experience this love
In the short span of their existence.

But you did.

This walkway of flowers
That you meandered through
day in and day out
Was just a piece of your happiness—
Just small instants
In a lifetime of bliss.

Reality is, love resides in a thought of the past,

Of a home and a love that lasted,
An amazing life lived,
An enrichment of reminiscence.

And may all of the breaths you took,
And the ticks of the clock,
All of the steps on your path
And all of the laughs
All of the kisses and all of the tears of contentment
Come flooding your mind
Every time you think of—

The walkway of flowers that garnished your path
To your home adored, your shelter of love
That you will carry with you now
All the days of your life
In your heart and in your mind.

And out of nowhere, it will sneak up on you
As you walk along other paths of flowers
You'll remember the time of your life
In your home you'll always hold dear.

And a smile will come upon your face
You'll embrace the nostalgia—
Close your eyes and remember
All the moments time stood still
On your journey through your walkway of flowers.

I genuinely love hearing the stories of my clients and helping them reach their real estate goals. Some sell out of necessity, some buy for a brighter future. Some make very hard decisions to move on to a new chapter in life. So many reasons and so many wonderful people met and memories made.

During most of the time that I have sold real estate, I have also had other things going on. I just sold my store that sold CBD and other cannabis-related products and am looking for my next side gig. But I'm a firm believer in fate, and at one point, I worked for a company—remember the one that said I was too comma happy in my writing?

Yeah, that one.

Well, this company was a sort of real estate tech company where I did a lot of things, from writing articles to coaching real estate agents. Here, one agent I was coaching decided that she no longer needed our services because she was opening a cannabis store. And that very moment birthed my next stepping stone; I went to Florida with her for a conference and ultimately opened my own store.

It's not always easy. In this journey, I've actually opened two stores, and then the COVID-19 pandemic hit. I had to close one store down due to declining sales, and I had to move the other because it was inside of a mall that closed for months due to COVID-19.

I ultimately decided to sell my store because originally I ran my store as an affiliate, but then the company decided to turn into a franchise, and we all know I don't like to be told what to do. My hope for selling this store was to start another business that I totally create for myself and maybe even work on starting a nonprofit that speaks so dear to me. I used my profits from the store to buy land very close to my home that is zoned for commercial use. It is currently going through environmental studies and other things to prepare for development. Excited about what's coming!

I'm always taking detours and closing roads down

completely on my travels. But it is always done with intention and for the greater good of what is to come. I've learned that these roadblocks I faced, and these detours I intentionally or even forcefully took, perhaps weren't roadblocks and detours after all. Perhaps they were just the path I was always meant to take. It seems the road I've traveled always was meant for me.

Prior to getting into ownership of a cannabis store, I ran a limo company. It was FUN! I had a limo and a party bus, and on many occasions when the vehicles weren't in use by clients, we would go for joy rides as a family. Every day was a party!

I am constantly growing, evolving, and dabbling in different things, all at the same time. My new obsession is learning and investing in the stock market, mainly in crypto and the cannabis industry. While I am surely no expert, I've experienced some good fortune when it comes to investing. Sometimes I win, sometimes I lose. But I have definitely had more luck than not.

Sometimes, I wander and do other things in my down moments. Sometimes, I enjoy letting passive income work while I take time off. This will be me for the rest of my life, and I am content.

Either way, the living I make for myself has often been used as a means to help others.

"We make a living by what we get, but we make a life by what we give."
—Winston Churchill

And while I love helping anyone in need, I really like to focus on our youth because I believe we have the power to change an entire generation by teaching our young people to accept and to give love and to do and be good.

By teaching our youth about how to find their own savage

happiness that they can exude onto others, we have the potential to change the world!

And if you don't think this is true, think about this. The Bible was written thousands of years ago. That's a long-ass time! And still, somehow words that were written so long ago and experiences biblical people went through are speaking to me in the here and now. Reading some of these things at just the time that I need to hear it makes me feel like God orchestrated these words, or that song, or this friend to come in contact with me just when I needed it. That's a damn good purpose. To be the person someone needs at just the right time and place right here, right now. And one day, years in the future, someone may pick up this book at just the right time and gather something that they will carry with them into a more savage happy life. UBUNTU. I am who I am because of all of the connections I have made, the paths I have crossed, and the humanity found in others. I am molded and shaped by all of my life encounters and I wouldn't be me without the people I have experienced life with.

Self-Reflection:

1. What have you defined as your purpose? This is kind of a mix between what you love, what you are good at, what you do for a living, and what those around you need.

____

____

____

____

____

____

____

____

____

____

2. Look back to question five of Chapter 3's Self-Reflection. Reflect on the immediate, short-term, and long-term goals you have set for yourself. These goals will ultimately serve as a path to your purpose. Are you on track? If not, what is hindering you? What are the goals you are struggling with, and what do you feel is the barrier or obstacle preventing you from going forward? Dig deep because this may mean that you have to alter your goal and go down a different path. Sometimes, it means just finding a different way to continue down this path.

3. What are your passions? What means so much to you that you are willing to work hard for, even BATTLE for, being the warrior you are?

This can include items from the list you made in the last chapter. Or we can get more literal and say that passion is something we are willing to experience suffrage for. What goal have you set for yourself that you feel so strongly about that you are willing to suffer or sacrifice in order to bring it to fruition? There is energy in writing things down, so list those items here and put all of your energy into them.

____

____

____

____

____

4. For each item you mention in question two as holding you back, brainstorm ways to get past it and back on course. Be thoughtful in creating this list of things you can do to satisfy yourself so you can fill your cup over and over again. Think about what you turn to when you need to refresh your outlook or cope with something causing you to deter off track. Write your thoughts in this space.

____

____

____

____

____

5. What do you do to stay on track with your goals?

____

____

____

____

____

____

6. And finally, my last suggestion for this topic—create a vision board for your immediate, short-term, and long-term goals. For me, I focus on mental, emotional, physical, and spiritual health when creating my goals. You can either draw your pictures, look some up on the computer to print, or even flip through a magazine to find them. Place these vision boards somewhere you can see, and dream about it every single day.

There are also virtual vision boards you can create through apps that you can access from your phone whenever you need to.

I would love to see some of the vision boards that you have created! If you are up to it, please share them with me at commahappyenjoythepause@gmail.com.

____
____
____
____
____
____

Don't just write your goals once a year. Evaluate them yearly, quarterly, monthly, weekly, and daily. Assess your passions on a regular basis. Work your way, step by step, day by day, to a kick-ass, savage, happy life with your purpose in mind.

chapter 6

THOU SHALT FIND YOUR GOALS AND
PASSIONS TO HELP OTHERS

I learned through the birth of my daughter that I have no pain receptors in my uterus...or something mysterious. It's really a phenomenon. The medical professionals don't really understand why I don't feel birth pains. In fact, I don't have any feeling. They have to tell me when I am having a contraction and when I need to push. Otherwise, I wouldn't know.

My son was my first born, but I was young and dumb and took advice from others and had an epidural before the real labor even happened in fear of feeling the pain I heard so much about. I heard all about the intolerable suffering a woman's body goes through in order to bring life into this world. I had preeclampsia during my son's pregnancy, so I had a bit of an emergency with his delivery and had to be induced. The epidural was awful in itself because I had months of back issues from it. I didn't want that with my next pregnancy, so I delivered my daughter natu-rally and have delivered every baby after in the same manner.

Because of this discovery that I don't feel labor pains, I decided that this was some sort of gift! And if it was a gift, I wanted to use it to help the world! After doing some research, I discovered I could be a surrogate. I could have babies for other people—their baby, my body.

To be honest, I ended up being a surrogate the first time because I was moving to Pennsylvania, and I wanted the opportunity to spend some quality time with my children. So I decided to begin my college courses (which I conducted online) and carry babies for other people as a means to support my children along with the GI Bill payment I received from the military for attending school. This allowed me the opportunity to stay with my children, go to school, and provide for my children while bettering myself.

<u>Familial Unity</u>

How many heartbeats
Had rhythm in me?
A pulse of a different beat.

Some bear my lineage,
Some have none,
I was just the carrier with no relation.

But their blood flowed through my body,
I cared for them as if they were mine
For the short time they inhabited me.

And upon delivering, I returned them to
The arms that loved them so, so much
That they gave up control and trusted me
To bear them their child
They had hoped for their whole lives
But couldn't conceive
-—What a huge responsibility!—

To aid with life
With new beginnings
for others to reap.
And in the end, I know
It will come full circle back to me
For we reap what we sow...

And each new first breath I witnessed,
Each new mother or fathers' happy tears,
Each new family I helped build
Bit by bit helped mold me.

What a journey it has been
I am so fulfilled.
What an opportunity
To be the hand of kindred love
For familial unity...

My husband has always allowed me to be me. I went directly from our very first date to have the procedure of my first surrogacy journey in 2008. In all, I was a surrogate mother seven times, resulting in seven live births. Of these, four of the babies carried my genes, and I acted as a traditional surrogate. Four times, I was a gestational surrogate and was only the vehicle to bring the babies to their parents. I delivered one set of twins, and one pregnancy ended in termination.

With the sweet girl whose pregnancy was terminated, she had only grown half of her heart. If it had been the other half, she could have had a procedure to correct it. However, she was missing the wrong half of her heart. The doctor told us she had a

0% chance of living once she was born and the heart chambers switched over. I got a second opinion because I had a hard time accepting this as her fate. When their opinion was the same, her parents chose to terminate her life, and I obliged.

I don't like to use the term abortion. I didn't have the procedure that ripped her apart out of my womb, but I did take a drug that put me in labor early in order to deliver a baby girl at 22 weeks, knowing she wouldn't survive.

It was very difficult for me, as I was alone in the hospital and had to see her off to exhale her last breath. I was a coward. I couldn't witness it myself. I didn't have the heart for it. She was cooing and making sounds. I was told that at 22 weeks, she wouldn't even breathe on her own. And yet, she did. After I held her, spoke to her and kissed her forehead, I sent her off with the nurse to take her final breath.

For a small moment, I was hopeful that the doctors were wrong and that she would make it. But the nurse came in and told me she had passed peacefully. I think she lived 32 minutes. I named her Aahna. Her father and the donor egg were of Indian descent, and Aahna means "to exist" in Hindi. I'm not sure if her parents gave her a name, but I decided this would be a perfect name to retell her story by.

<u>Sweet Aahna, You Existed</u>
Biologically you weren't mine, but I'm grieving nonetheless
I don't know why life happens this way
It wasn't my decision to make
I wish I could just pretend it away—
But I can't. **You existed**

Your life was cut short and I share the blame
You existed and I must acknowledge my shame

You lived for such a brief time,
And you departed just the same,
But **you existed**, sweet Aahna, you were here.

While I took the drug to bring you to life,
To come to the surface, to breathe in this air
To leave my body and lay face to face
Knowing once you arrived you would face your fate
But for just a brief time, **you existed**.

My actions aren't what did you in.
I'm comforted in knowing there was no other choice,
For you were cursed with just half a heart,
And even if I regarded your growing inside of my womb
You still wouldn't have survived
And I cut short your suffering, sweet Aahna,
I honor your being.

You existed, sweet Aahna,
You inhabited this earth
In time and space, for only minutes
We were touched by your grace.
Even though I was just your surrogate,
You had meaning, sweet Aahna.

This wasn't how your parents wished it would be.
Their visions of you are now just memories.
You're remembered beloved, a treasured impression,
A being released into the ether.
You'll always exist in spirit, Sweet Aahna.

I'm sorry I couldn't change your circumstance

It was I who was with you in the end.
I held you in my arms,
I kissed your head and saw you off.
I hold high regard for the short life you lived
Your existence is cherished, sweet Aahna.

Dear Aahna, you lived a brief moment in time,
But you'll always inhabit a space in my mind.
Your existence is always engraved in me
I'll forever wonder what could have been.
You'll be remembered by your innocence.
You existed, sweet Aahna. You were here.

As you see, using my passion to help others sometimes led to hard times. But because of my life experiences I usually handle hurt differently than most. It's ironic that my uterus handles pain differently and so do I as a whole.

But my passion has also led to many happy times, too. I still get updates from some of the biological parents. Some choose not to, and that is okay too. It is their journey; I only walked it for that brief time with them.

Tim was with me through all of my surrogacy journeys, and for most of them, he was even in the delivery room with me, even though he turned ghostly white and had to sit down each time. But I won't go there. HA!

I was born with a hiatal hernia that caused a lot of medical issues for me as a baby. Finally, at ten months old, I had it operated on. Then, several years ago, I was having some medical issues, and after several hospital visits and tests, we found out that the hernia came back. I had to have it repaired again, and unfortunately, I had a lot of scar tissue built up that caused some minor complications after surgery. As a result, and after much contemplation and discussion with my husband, we thought I should switch my focus from delivering babies through surrogacy to nurturing babies through foster care. So, Tim and I got licensed through a local foster care agency.

Just a few days before my hernia surgery, we received a call from the agency asking if we were able to take in our very first placement. And then, the day after our new placement came and settled in, I decided to shave my head for St. Baldrick's to help them raise money for children's cancer research. They are a nonprofit that aids in funding research for a brighter outcome and future for children with cancer. (Visit http://www.stbaldricks.org for more info.) It was a whirlwind of a week for us, to say the least. It was cool, though, because our first placement was a female who struggled with gender identity and also had a bald head.

We have had many teens through our home since, all with a variety of circumstances that molded them. We are a stepping stone when they come to us, and our goal is to be a permanent foundation for them even after they grow up and move on.

We have had children come to us so depressed that they didn't want to function. They had no self-esteem and wouldn't stand up for themselves. They believed what they heard, and they were broken based on their young life experiences. Some struggled with the basics because they were so consumed with things they had no business being exposed to. Furthermore, some came needing assistance with all facets of life. We have decided to be their voice and to help them find the strength inside themselves. We decided to step in and show them what love is and what life can look like. After all, children are our future.

This was the first poem I penned for a foster child...our very first foster child. And to see them now and where they are at right now in life is amazing! They made a hard decision once leaving here to go to Job Corp. I was able to visit and be there for them during this time. And when they graduated from the program, they got an awesome position in security. I couldn't be more proud!

You Are My Child (Fostering a Teen)
My priorities lie in loving you
And demonstrating how to love.
You may have never seen it before,
You may have never felt it.
It's not just in words, but in action.
But don't distress, I will show you what to do.
I am your mom.

It doesn't matter what they decide
Is the best place for you to be.
Regardless of how little or how much time you have with us,
As long as you are here,
We will show you unity.
You are worthy to belong.
We are your family.

You are just a child.
You shouldn't carry the weight of the world on your shoulders.
So much of what weighs you down
Is not yours to carry.
Let it go, and be free of the burden only meant for me.
That is a part of my job, too.
I'll carry that weight for you.

I'm here to show you how to act appropriately
And how to care for yourself.
For there will be a time
When I won't be able to call your name,
To wake you in the morning.
I won't be here to remind you to clean behind your ears
And wear deodorant and brush your teeth.
And do your homework, and do your chores,
Create a resume, and find a job.
Go to bed early so you can get up
And start all over again.
Soon, this will become second nature for you.
As you figure life out,
And you learn to be productive in society.

I will show you how to live in a sometimes-cold world
And how to be the warmth that you yourself need.
For I will not always be right beside you.
But my hope is that you will always look back and see
That you held the power within yourself
The entire time!
When you realize this, you will be free!

And in your freedom,
You will learn that others will depend on you
To help them through their darkest hours.
After all, the goal in life is to find peace within ourselves
So that we may shine for others to see
The goodness they have hidden inside themselves.
It's a beautiful cycle!!

I already see you leaving your footprint

As you figure out who you are.
You can be anything you want to be!
You can go anywhere! Do anything!
Live out your dreams!

And when you hit a hindrance, or feel overwhelmed, it's okay.
Collect yourself, and start over.
Every day is a new day
And a new chance to do tremendous things.
For you are deserving.
I recognize your greatness, and I hold high regard for you.
I have faith that you have it within yourself
To love and to make this world better.
You are distinguished.

I know this, because you are my child...
You are a part of me.
You will always be able to call this home.
We are your family.
Even when you're gone.

I get so intertwined with what goes on in my life, it becomes a part of my being. All these little pieces of each step I have taken are sewn together to create me. Every choice I make, every encounter I cross, it all defines me, and without it, I wouldn't be me.

And with every child that comes through my home, I see myself in them. I can pinpoint something I went through that relates to something they have gone through. When they struggle, I struggle with them. I relate because I've been that broken child who just longed for love. I've been so depressed I couldn't leave the bed. I've had times when I was weak and had no self-worth. And I worked hard to get myself out of that pit. I strive to have a hand in helping each child who comes through my doors get themselves through their own struggles so they can then help the next person.

Some of the kids come to our home so grown that they are rebellious because they feel they don't need us. They've had to raise themselves most of their lives. They've lived their lives in survival mode and have no idea what it feels like to have others look out for them. House rules are foreign and take away their freedom. They do not realize how freeing it is to have family, a place to help care for and come back to when in need, and siblings to look out for. They can't comprehend how much stronger we are when we have others watching our backs for us. Life was never designed to spend every waking moment fighting. It's meant to always have people in your corner.

The child I wrote this poem for actually left our home a few months before turning eighteen. The agency felt it was best that they leave because of the situation we were in with them, and they went to stay with another foster family for the last couple of months. And now, years later, we still chat on Facebook. I still help them get through some stuff, including taking them to look at a rental property to make sure it is a safe place. Even when life happens and times get hard...even when words are said and things are done...we are still family, and I won't turn my back on them.

The Spark Ignited the Bonfire

You're reckless and savage, wild and untamed
Your vision is blurred...
but your essence possesses an internal flame.
A fire burning for all the wrong reasons,
A lawless rebel in search of freedom.

But what is the cost of this freedom, you ask?
The promise to represent yourself. Make your own decisions.
Create your own rules, your own regulations.
Seems like such a small task...

A small price to pay, or so it may seem
But is it worth sacrificing your dreams?
As you work endlessly to provide a life that
You lose track of time from, and next thing you know,
Your life has been lived...exhausted and wasted.

And then, what's the point when you're living in survival mode?
As you are weighed down by an insane workload?
Your minutes are full, you can't even breathe.
There's so much to do but you must believe.
Believe in yourself and in a better future.

You're a whirlwind, unsettled, eccentric, and feral,
But you're fierce and relentless...know that there will be
Hardships along your entire journey, but you won't slow down
You are your own army...

An army of one, an overcomer, a warrior.
You have strength in your thoughts.
Now, have control of your actions.
That is where your real power is.

I urge you to aim your aggressions, your determinations
At bettering yourself and your situation.
Don't limit yourself, keep growing and learning,
Fight for yourself, let that fire keep burning...

You are in control of your own contentment.
Release your bond of circumstance, don't live in your past.
Create the most beautiful life that you can.
Don't worry so much about what comes tomorrow.
Slow down and breathe and live for the moment.

Don't change. Be impulsive.
Just aim it at your pursuit of a promising future.
Have passion and purpose and reach your potential.
Continue to live on the edge of the world.
But channel your energy into your advancement.

You can be anything that you want to be.
You were always designed to be free.
Free in your mind, free in your spirit,
Inspired in greatness, inside you are fearless.

The world's not against you. It's not a bad thing
To have someone accountable for the choices you make.
You are a visionary, wired in worth despite what you've been
through.
Your strength says it all. You were born for this.
So go out there and accomplish your purpose.
Your options are boundless.
Keep making progress.

You are a reflection of the life that you lived.
Learn from it, grow, get out of the dark...
And in the end, have the biggest bonfire
That ignited with just that initial spark...

And let the fire grow bigger than ever before...

This child really spoke to me. I spent my life raising myself and never wanted anyone to tell me what to do. I understood their need to lie to get what they wanted. I get why they felt like the truth would get them a "no," and "no" is not something they could handle at that moment. They are still trying to work through this hard life. They are definitely still a work in progress, but I have total hope that once they figure it out, they will be unstoppable!

Some foster kids who came to us reminded me so much of me. They looked for love and acceptance in boys just as I did all throughout life. The child I wrote this poem for didn't talk to us much. They had a very bad attitude. They ran away and ran to the boys. Ultimately, they decided to leave our home to go to a group home because it was close to a boy they liked.

I can't even say anything because when you live a life in which you were given up on, left to fend for yourself, you establish a void and a need to fill that void.

<u>Think of Her…</u>

You don't have to run to this boy—then this boy—
then that boy—and that
Or send this photo—and that photo—
and this through Snapchat.
You don't have to show your midriff—your cleavage—
or your behind.
It's never too late to be redefined.

Love yourself, you're valuable…
Be radical in uncovering your worth, but also be rational.
You're better than that…

Aim for success, not material things
but happiness, a heart that rests.

Excel in school, not because someone told you to
But because it's what you need to do
To get to where you want to be in life.
Stabilize.

If you need help, always seek it,
But don't scheme and deceive in order to get it.
Be colorful in finding contentment,
But don't do it at the expense of someone else's enjoyment.

Have influence—yes!
But aim for positive impact...
You have the power to change the world around you—
and within you...
You are prompt and attentive to adapt to what life throws at you.

Just don't be swayed, and don't get in your own way.
Your future self will give many thanks
Think of her in the decisions you make.

Even if you're not where you want to be now,
You'll get there by putting your future self first.
Become immersed in loving yourself.
Something so important can't be left in the hands of anyone else.

Once you master the art of self-respect and self-devotion,
There's no limit to your self-promotion...
It's okay to feel important—
have pride in knowing you are someone special...

In the end, you are the only one with that authority…

Take care of your vessel and all of the treasure stored inside.
That is your duty. Your future self is noticing…

Be purposeful in your future success.
Every day is a new day, so if you mess up—it's okay!
Open your eyes and start again…and again…
Until you get to a place where you can begin
To offer yourself love and embrace.
And even a little pinch of grace.

We all deserve second chances.
And once you've mastered loving yourself,
There's no stopping you.
No circumstance will break you.

You'll realize you were qualified this entire time…
You're fortified!
Your future self will always look back and recognize
You had control all along…
and you had to endure everything you did
To get to the fulfillment of self-satisfaction…

Repeatedly seek progress—and be satisfied…
Your future self is applauding you…
Especially through your sacrifice and compromise
To continually consider what's best for you.

In this last poem, I feel like I was looking in the mirror and talking to myself. I've also been so angry at some of the shit I have had to endure. I've been mad at the world and mad that I didn't seem to make progress in some moments of my life. I'd get myself in situations to obtain attention, and afterward, I felt so bad about myself. But, oh, for a moment, I was on top of the world, and I had control of it.

I don't talk to this foster child as much as I'd like. I check in occasionally and send money when they need it. I'm available when they need me and love from a distance the rest of the time.

Some foster children came in here ready to tear the world down with their anger from what they had been through in their short lives. They were confused and didn't understand what they were experiencing. As they learned themselves, they became angry at how they were being treated and controlled.

One was particularly hard for me because they went back home. And while that is always the goal when able, I was worried for them. Since COVID-19 hit, no one has had eyes on them. But I recently heard they and their mom moved in with their gramma, so my heart is overjoyed that they are rekindling their relationship. I send positive light and love to their sweet spirit so that they can find rest as they grow in this world.

<u>Be Satisfied</u>

You came in like a hurricane,
determined to tear down everything.
After all, with your surroundings flattened, ruined, out of view,
You will tower over all, with nothing else to see...except you.
What gloom to be the only one standing.

But the truth is when you try to bring others down,
you are already beneath them.
Burning at their feet, a volcano—trying to erupt.
How grand would it be still
if you could aid in the feat of lifting others up?

That's how you rise...
releasing the innocent from being condemned.

Escaping your wrath. Those uninvolved, the casualties.
Just let them be!
And focus on the possibilities.
Be the tree with vines extended down,
Draw others out of your murky pit...your mercy shown.
You will restore, after all you are life—you are the tree...

You will rise and overcome if you use your influence
to help those in need.
Let your chaos succumb to the fire inside. Aim to destroy no more
And simply restore those all around you.
You have the power to wage war
On inequality...swaddle yourself among other kind trees
and plant those seeds.

You are enough, just as you are. Explore yourself.
You already know.
You are the calm. Feel the peace buried inside.
Let it arise and may it reside...
Be sick no more...shut out the plague...
be whole, and let your goodness show.

You have it in you and you know it to be true.
You've already started the process...
You're standing up for yourself, you're very wise.
Your great name means "object of devotion,"
but be careful where your devotion lies
Be true and devoted to yourself, don't settle for less...

You'll figure it out, how much you are worth…
And in your vastness, you can cultivate your environment—you
can win!
Be more alive than you've ever been!
Make this life count, be one with the earth…

And in the end, you are good—your soul is kind
You've seen a lot, you aren't blind!
You can't unlive the things you've been through,
But know that it wasn't you.

You did nothing wrong, so shuffle your cards
and keep on playing!
And until then, I'll be praying…
Knowing that you'll be left with battle scars…

But don't feel defeated,
Carry them with pride because you survived!
You are the mighty, mighty tree…
Be satisfied…

In all of life, just be satisfied…

This child grew so much in the small amount of time that they lived with us. They used to hold a lot inside, afraid of hurting those they loved. And while holding it in, they exploded on those who didn't deserve it. But they found their voice and learned to talk about how they felt.

Some of the foster children who have come to our home are almost adults in age but never had a childhood. When they get to our place, they struggle with preparing for adult life. They just want to be a kid and learn. They aren't ready to grow up so quickly...but boy, does eighteen come quick for them sometimes.

This was written for a teen who came to us with a lot on their shoulders. They had learned somewhere in life to manipulate to get just their basic needs met. So many times in their stay here, they fought when they could have just asked. I hope we planted seeds in that department. We've heard from them just a couple of times since they left our home, but ultimately, they have chosen no contact for some time now. I hope they read this and decide to reach out and continue a relationship. We want to be a solid foundation of hope and love.

Love is All Around You

You're smart, you're brilliant...
Insightful, ingenious.
You're bold and bright
And keen to what's right.

Oh, how I've imagined you
Using these proficiencies
For the good of all mankind.

I know you're still growing into yourself
And exploring a confidence of new heights.
My hope is once you've established
A faith in yourself, a certainty within,
Your guard will go down, you'll transform the fight.

The world has been on your side all along.
There's no need to bring down others
In order to advance your gain and attain
Everything you desire. There's a better way!

You mastered alternative perceptions,
Your schemes and deceptions,
The games you've played,
The tricks you engineered and arranged.

The plots you've devised,
They've been your way of life,
Even after you left,
But I know in my heart, you have the force within
To be the light!

I know it hurt you that I had to set boundaries
For myself. I had no choice.
You're canny and can find weaknesses in others
And feed off of it. Your power grew
With each lie you told.
As each stunt unfolded.
And each scenario you brewed.

I must make sure you know, though,
That you have such a warmth in you.
You have the potential to add positive weight.
Your influence is magic.
Regulate your circumstances.

Advocate for your better good
By demonstrating your worth.
You're equipped with a suited mind,
A gifted intellect, inventive thoughts
With so much to give to humankind.

My heart and soul send positive energy to you

Each and every day, I pray for you.
I have so much faith in you.
Your dreams and ambitions are at your fingertips.
From a distance, I am loving you…

I want so much to be here for you.
Maybe one day you can open your view
To see I was really looking out for you.
All this time and in my own way…
And if you ever pick up the phone and reach out to me,
I will answer in a heartbeat.

There's an insane potential for greatness,
You possess mental competence.
I invoke you to look inside yourself,
Unearth your strength and your voice,
And use them for good.

Good merit is inside you. Discover this part of you.
And you will be unstoppable.
Obtaining your every wish and desire is possible
If you just work hard for it.
And you don't have to do it alone.
I'm here to lift you up in love.

Love surrounds you in this big world…
It's all around.

I can't say that I blame them for their survival responses. If I had been through some of the stuff they have, I may have reacted the same in certain situations throughout life. In fact, if you recall, there was a time in my life where I did play a victim and used manipulation tactics when I was desperate for love. I cut my wrist with a butter knife to produce blood in hopes of getting sympathy from my ex-husband. So I get it...but there's a better way.

This was written for our most recent placement in our home. They just moved into their own apartment a couple of months ago. Their "normal" wasn't really normal, so we battled with monitoring appropriate behavior so it didn't affect the others in the home. They have had so much growth since coming here, and I am so proud of their progress. They are working on their GED, they have a job, and have come so far in life. We talk often, and they are always evolving and are receptive to learning and growing.

Faith in You

The things you have seen, what you've been through
Doesn't make you. It doesn't define you.
Life has been hard for you, there's no denying
It has at times even been horrifying...

But here you are, fighting for a chance,
Given a new circumstance.
Torn between wanting independence, adulthood,
Or finally enjoying the opportunity of a childhood...

That's definitely a hard thing to decide...
Society expects you to overcome and uprise.
But we are here to help you learn and grow,
And I really need you to know.

You can't look around you for approval...
Look inside—that's where true acceptance lies.

Once you accept yourself completely,
You will find a confidence so deep...

Nothing will stop you or get in your path.
Soon, your anger and your wrath
Will turn to self-love and the need for success
When you focus on living, less stress, less mess...

Don't let what you've been through
keep your heart cold.
Stop being mean to everyone around you,
It will end up taking a toll on them and you.

I know you've seen a lot,
And your choice of language, music, what you watch,
Reflect your emotional disconnect
Cussing, murder, provocative sex,
But it's not your fault. It's all you saw...

You've grown so much...
Keep up the good fight for life,
push towards your goals...
You can do it! We have faith in you.

And we will always be beside you,
Rooting for you, guiding you, getting you through...
World, get ready!
What you set your mind to, you will do...
And we have all the faith in you.

One thing is true—for every child that comes through our
home, whether they stay with us, age out, go back home, or

whatever their circumstance is, each deserves permanency and stability. They all deserve a chance to be a child, to live in peace, to be taken care of while learning how to take care of themselves, to explore life and not have the weight of the world hanging over them at such a young age. They deserve love and support, guidance, the freedom to fall, and the assurance that they will have help getting back on their feet. They deserve a permanent foundation to which they can always return when they are in need.

Permanency

Everyone deserves permanency
Someone to love...stability...
The ability to rest our heads
Under a roof, in our own beds...

To have warm air in the winter, cold air when it's hot.
To have necessities...shouldn't even be a thought.

To take care of ourselves and rely on no one...
Not focused on survival,
Knowing when the day is done
We will not unravel...

To thrive on our own and earn everything we have...
Food, water, electricity, no fear of someone taking it...
Because you are in control of your life,
Only relying on yourself, determined to make it...

You are living the definition of security
Free from threat of losing it all
On your own two feet
Doing what they said couldn't be done.

They said you would fall...
BUT LOOK AT YOU NOW!

At this point, the purpose of life kicks in.
You meet someone in need of a hand
They just need a shove in the right direction...
And here you are...to help them get a fresh start,
Supporting them off their knees,
Guiding them until they can do their part...
SHOWING THEM THE WAY
As someone once did for you.
Just until they come to a place where they can get through...

You can help them take that first step,
A foundation for transitioning...
You have your life together; you are able to offer some relief...
Small support...just enough,
So when times get rough, they won't give up...

And that is the circle of giving;
Kindness and love go such a long way
To help a person
Get to a place of permanency...

We give our children that come to us the space to live and figure themselves out. Before going out and facing this big, mean world, we are here to help them get their shit together. We remain here after they depart, regardless of the circumstances. There isn't anything they could do to stop us from caring for them, and we make sure they know that love is love. We are family. That is my purpose, and to be honest, they are fulfilling a purpose in being my family, too. I always joke and say I do this because I want a lot of people at my funeral celebrating the life I have lived, wearing bright, colorful clothes. But the truth is, I just really love having people here while I am still living who I can care for.

Our story is still being played out, and we still continue to foster. Every day is a new day full of fun and challenges, and I wouldn't have it any other way. For some, we are just a seed planted, for others we are the whole damn tree...but each child who comes to our home was meant to be here. Periodt.

Together with our kids, we have fed the homeless and handed out survival bags. I use my love of crocheting to make scarves and blankets in the winter for the homeless—anything I am able to do to brighten their day. Sometimes, we do this through a nonprofit that hands these items out on specific days, and sometimes we hit the streets and hand them out ourselves.

I do make sure if we are going out in the community that we are doing so in a group as I put the safety of my children first at all times. I'm aware of how desperation can change someone. But at the end of the day, when we have spent time giving, helping others and supplying others with hope, we have a bigger appreciation for life.

I genuinely believe the purpose of our talents, hobbies, gifts, and passions is to use them to help others. Giving is receiving. And when you give, you begin a cycle in others to pay it forward. My goal is to make at least one person smile each and every day. And I urge you, every day, do something for someone else with intention. It is healing. And as the good Audrey Hepburn said, "As you grow older, you will discover that you have two hands— one for helping yourself, the other for helping others." Helping yourself is important, but there's nothing better than the joy of helping others. Get yourself to a point of self-actualization, and then reach down to those around you and help them. It's that simple.

Self-Reflection:

1. In the last chapter, we discussed your passions and how they affect your goals, which leads to your purpose. Describe your passions, your hobbies, likes, and dislikes below. How do these make you feel? Usually, we give more meaning when we utilize the gifts that mean the most to us. Which are your favorites and why? Put a circle around your favorites.

____

____

____

____

____

____

2. How can you use your goals and passions to help others? This can be as simple as writing letters to the lonely if you like to write or babysitting for someone to try to find a job when you enjoy children. It can be as complex as devoting a portion of your paycheck to help a single mother feed her children and put a roof over the family's head or spending every morning growing a garden to feed the homeless. What is your superpower, and how can you use it to save one soul or the world?

____

____

____

____

____

____

3. Make a list of things you can do for others today.

One thing I wish I would have done throughout life is keep a journal and track some of the things I have done to help others or make them smile, and maybe even go back and write responses so I can monitor what works best. If you are feeling adventurous, start a kindness journal!

____

____

____

____

____

____

chapter 7

LIST OF WAYS TO PAY IT FORWARD/RANDOM ACTS OF KINDNESS

We have talked about creating a list of things that make US happy and doing something from this list every day. And we have been talking about our goals and passions and ultimately our purpose, and how I believe that everything about our makeup is designed to be used to help other people, from our gifts, hobbies, likes, all the way to our purpose.

So it makes sense that I would then create a list of things to do to help others. Below is MY list of things I do to pay it forward or make someone else's day.

When possible, while choosing an act of kindness, make a card to accompany your act of kindness and ask the person you have helped to also PAY IT FORWARD. Mine is below, but you can do a random act of kindness in honor of someone and put their name on the card or really change it up any way you wish. The idea is that we can make a difference and really change the world by giving and receiving kindness to and from strangers.

UBUNTU.

1. Pay for the food of the person behind you at the drive-through or the table beside you at a restaurant.

2. Pay for the person behind you at the toll booth.

3. Make survival packages and hand them out to the homeless or leave near a homeless shelter, especially during the winter. Some ideas to place in the package are:

- Socks
- Scarves
- Toothpaste and toothbrushes
- Feminine products
- Comb
- Deodorant
- Baby wipes
- Gift cards to restaurants
- Snacks

- Bottles of water
- Anything else that you can think of and fit in a gallon size bag.
- Or if you are able to find some cheap backpacks to place those items in, that would be even better! Then they can use the backpacks as they move throughout the day.

4. Buy a meal for a homeless person.

5. Give a warm coat to a homeless person or a gift card to allow them to pick out a new coat or shoes.

6. Use your talent to help others. For instance, I like to crochet, so I crochet blankets for delivery hospitals, blankets for animal shelters, blankets for homes that help those with abuse or addiction, scarves for the homeless, and other projects.

7. Don't cast judgment on those with addiction. Help them with their recovery by educating yourself about addiction and how to support them without enabling them. Minister to them. Help them find resources.

8. Compliment a stranger.

9. Smile at a stranger.

10. Let someone go in front of you at the grocery store checkout.

11. Return someone's grocery cart.

12. Use reusable bags at the grocery store, or if you use their bags, recycle the paper and return the plastic to their recycling center.

13. Use reusable water bottles.

14. Help someone load their groceries into their car at the grocery store.

15. Hold the door open for a stranger.

16. Visit hospice, a nursing home, senior center, or retirement home and spend time with someone who may not be alive tomorrow. This includes those you love, and those you don't

know. Some have no one. Call in and get on the schedule to visit. Maybe bring your pet, or coloring book, and crayons to do an activity. Your time and thought is needed and appreciated.

17. Volunteer at a battered women's shelter.

18. Volunteer at an animal shelter or donate supplies to an animal shelter.

19. Volunteer at a homeless shelter.

20. Volunteer with the Special Olympics. http://www.specialolympics.org

21. Volunteer at Habitat for Humanity. http://www.habitat.org

22. Donate blood http://www.redcross.org or donate plasma (the liquid component of blood that takes nutrients, hormones and proteins to the areas of the body that need it).

23. Recycle. Anything you can keep out of the landfill, do. Plastics, glass, cans, etc. You can even take your Walmart bags back to Walmart and they will reuse them.

24. Take shorter showers, turn off the sink water while brushing your teeth, turn lights off when not in use, conserve energy, conserve water, be conservative in the resources you use.

25. Get involved in the Big Brothers/Big Sisters program. http://www.bbbs.org or https://www.bigbrobigsis.com.

26. Become a foster parent.

27. Be a surrogate. Okay, not everyone can do this, but some can!

28. Volunteer to coach a kid sporting event.

29. Share your umbrella in the rain, or if you pitch a tent at a sporting event, share that to help block the sun.

30. Organize a carpool. Help other parents get their kids to sporting events, etc.

31. When you are spring cleaning, give your items to someone who needs it.

32. Make a care package for people in the military.

33. Make a difference. Contribute to society. Join the military or

do public works (do things for the community, even if you get paid for it).

34. Adopt a Soldier, especially at Christmas time through programs like www.americasadoptasoldier.org, www.soldiersangels.org, www.operationshoebox.com, and more. You can also go to http://www.honortroops.org, which sends care packages to those deployed.

35. Adopt a family in need and help them, guide them, mentor them. You can do this through the church, www.doinggoodtogether.org, www.christmasfamilyadoption.org and more.

36. Add change to someone's expired meter.

37. Tape a dollar with a note on a vending machine.

38. Leave quarters at the laundromat.

39. Buy someone's coffee. Leave money at the register, and tell the teller to pay for the next person and put the rest in the tip jar.

40. Offer cold drinks in the summer and hot drinks in the winter to delivery drivers, especially if you are anything like me and buy EVERYTHING from Amazon!

41. Grow a garden and donate a portion of it to those in need.

42. Tip well (taxi drivers, waiter/waitress, Doordash drivers, etc.).

43. Give up your seat on a crowded bus, train, etc.

44. When you see a soldier, a teacher, someone in the medical field, clergy, a police officer, a firefighter, or anyone else in the serving career, thank them for their service and sacrifices.

45. Pay for the meal of someone in a serving career.

46. Clean out books and donate them to the library.

47. Leave a copy of a really good book you have read somewhere for someone else to enjoy it.

48. Buy local.

49. Pick up trash in public areas, parks, along the road, etc.

50. Send a note to someone to thank them for changing your life.

51. I'm a bad driver, so I appreciate this one: let a driver merge into your lane.

52. Make donations to organizations and causes that mean something to you.

53. Instead of gifts for your birthday, wedding, etc, request others to donate to your causes in your honor.

54. Offer to babysit for a single mother, a new family, or someone who just needs a break.

55. Help with an inner-city project.

56. Shovel someone's snow, mow their grass, rake their leaves, etc.

57. Give a lottery ticket to a stranger.

58. Hold a can drive and collect nonperishable items for a charity in need.

59. Refer businesses to others, and form a group so your friends can meet and share business ideas and referrals. Also use social media to get your friend's business out there! Help grow your local businesses and support small business owners.

60. Help an entrepreneur in an underserved community by offering some of your funds as a loan on http://www.kiva.org.

61. When you have a positive experience with an employee, ask for management and let them know.

62. Leave testimonials and online reviews for good business experiences.

63. Adopt a pet.

64. Go to as many charity events as possible.

65. Volunteer at a food bank.

66. Volunteer at a fire department.

67. Grow your hair and donate it to Locks of Love. http://www.locksoflove.org.

68. Cut your hair and raise money for St. Baldricks. http://www.stbaldricks.org.

69. Become an organ donor. You can register for this through the DMV.

70. Help someone write a resume or find a job.

71. Treat your neighbors. Bake them cookies, or a meal, or go play games with them. Being neighborly is important to our well being.

72. Be a designated driver to allow someone to go out and have fun. Be there to make sure they arrive home safely.

73. Invite someone over for the holidays.

74. Help someone move. As a real estate agent, I run into this all of the time. I even have a trailer that I use JUST to help my clients move.

75. Find a public wish list on Amazon and send a stranger a gift.

76. Send holiday cards. If you missed the holidays, just send out "thinking of you" cards. With technology, many don't use snail mail anymore, and it is a nice surprise to receive something.

77. Help natural disaster victims.

78. If you see someone sitting alone when you are eating out, ask them if they would like to join you.

79. Offer someone a piece of gum.

80. Measure your carbon footprint and work on keeping it low. http://www.nature.org/greenliving/carboncalculator/index.htm.

81. Start a club of kindness or good deeds. Gather with a group of people and monthly and work as a group to do good for others. Use this list as a guide!

82. Don't know where to volunteer? Go to http://www.volunteermatch.com and let them help you!

83. Go to http://www.honortroops.org or http://www.troopster.com, both of which send care packages to those deployed.

84. Help feed those in need by volunteering with Meals on Wheels. https://www.mealsonwheelsamerica.org.

85. Shop at http://www.greatergood.com. They raise money for nonprofits that you support through your purchases.

86. Keep stuff out of the landfill by visiting http://www.freecycle.org.

87. Go to http://www.techfortroops.org, give old tech equipment to help veterans, and give back to your local veteran community.

88. Select your charitable organization on AmazonSmile, Kroger Community Rewards, and other charitable programs.

89. Find out how to become a CASA (Court Appointed Special Advocate) volunteer worker who advocates for children in foster care, at http://www.nationalcasagal.org.

90. Volunteer at http://www.crisistextline.com to help those going through a crisis anywhere from anxiety to suicidal thoughts.

91. Volunteer with http://www.gfwc.org (a women's club) to improve communities.

92. Plant a tree in someone's honor. Even more special, plant a fruit tree in a public place so the homeless can feed from it (with permission, of course).

93. Buy a small plot of land in the city and start a community garden so others who don't have land can grow their own food.

94. Give directions to someone who looks lost.

95. If you are a coupon cutter, cut some out and place them beside those items in the grocery store for others to enjoy.

96. Learn CPR and other life-saving measures. You never know when you just might need to use it.

97 When nonprofits are holding events like a charity walk, participate in it!

98. Donate unused frequent flier miles to nonprofits.

99. Take a shift at your local soup kitchen.

100. Donate your sick leave to someone in need at your office.

101. Bring in treats for coworkers, and be anonymous.

102. Read to your child's class.

103. Send in more school supplies for your child's class.

104. Attend events that your friends invite you to. They put a lot of time into that event.

105. Let your spouse sleep in and you pick up the morning routine.

106. Honestly there are so many places that need help. Just get out and volunteer! Pick your passion and help a cause. Autism Society, Leukemia Society, Smile Train, St. Jude's, World Pediatric Project, Reece's Rainbow, Operation Enduring Warrior, United Network of Organ Sharing, National Fallen Firefighter Foundation, National Police Foundation, the Orphan Care Network, Love Fosters Hope, We Will Speak, and so many other local and international nonprofits need your help. Pick one and help.

107. Make being kind a priority, and if someone ever asks how they can repay you, ask them to PAY IT FORWARD.

108. Don't forget to be kind to yourself! Take time for self-care. Get that pedicure, get a massage, listen to music, read a book. Whatever rejuvenates you. Make sure you are lifting yourself up so you have the energy to give to others.

I don't know about you, but the more I give, the better I feel about life. I am always excited to learn new ways to be kind or to make this world a better place, so if you come across any more ideas to pay it forward or conduct acts of kindness, please share them with me at commahappyenjoythepause@gmail.com.

1. Do you have a list you go by when you want to be kind to someone? If not, I encourage you to make your own list today! If the list above feels overwhelming, maybe start with just three things you can do to bring a smile to someone's face. As you conquer those three items, add three more to your list. Baby steps are always better than standing still.

____

____

____

____

____

2. Make it a goal to do something from this list every single day. It is good for your soul.

____

____

____

____

____

sheltering womb

chapter 8

THOU SHALT HAVE COMPASSION
BUT PROTECT THYSELF

As you learned, my father left when I was eight years old…he was gone for twenty years. No one heard from him. No one knew if he was alive. He basically disappeared from the face of this earth.

When I was living in Charlottesville as a single mother with my first child, I received a call from my mom saying my father contacted her, asking where I was and if he could contact me. I agreed. For a long while, we only wrote to each other and maybe had an occasional phone call. A lot of time passed, and there were a few discussions about him coming to visit, but it never happened.

Then, not long after I moved in with my husband (my then-boyfriend), I received a call from my father to pick him up at the Greyhound station. I wasn't ready to face that part of my life at the time, so Tim faced it for me and went to pick him up.

Tim is the most amazing man and always does what needs to be done. I think he felt good knowing that my father and I connected, but he is also my protector. The only time we really discuss the situation of my father being here is when he does things that hurt me. Then, Tim steps in and puts his foot down,

159

whether it is to put him in his place, to keep the serenity in my home, or to set the boundary and let him know that it won't continue. Tim has always been good at that.

My father lived with us for more than ten years upon his arrival, and we have cared for him all that time. I don't think there was ever even a discussion of if he would live with us. I think he just assumed that he would, and we just took on the responsibility.

At first, my father lived with us in our home for a while. He had to share a room with my oldest son because we didn't have a lot of space in our home. There was some awkward silence as we avoided discussing what happened so long ago when he left. At one point, I tried to talk to him about why he made the decisions he did, but it was clear he took no responsibility. We yelled at each other momentarily, and then I decided it wasn't worth fighting about. The damage was done, and at that point in my life, it didn't really matter what his reasons were. I just accepted that he probably did me a favor by leaving and not raising me.

Tim and I got married not long after my father came to live with us. I've always said I wasn't getting married until my father could walk me down the aisle. However, he wasn't there for my first wedding. Looking back now, I should have taken that as a sign that the marriage wouldn't have worked. But he was here to be a part of my wedding with Tim.

I don't know how my mother feels about him living here in Virginia. I'm sure it hurts her that he is around his grandkids and she lives far away. I've tried to get her to move here several times, but something is keeping her in Johnstown.

Once Tim and I got married, we decided to buy an RV and park Dad in the front yard. I had to get him out of my house and out of my calm, happy space. He stayed in the RV at the next house we moved to as well. At our last house, he stayed in a small room in the garage.

Our last home had an apartment above the garage, and I could have put him up there, but to be honest, I knew he would destroy it. We ended up taking a huge loss on the RV when we sold it because he sacked it pretty bad. I wasn't going to let that happen to the beautiful apartment.

He also used to eat with us every night. I felt obligated to keep him alive, and including him for dinner felt like a necessity to make sure he was able to eat. We even invited him with us when we ate out and covered his charge every time.

All of that ended during 2021, when he tried to cause drama within my home when he accused my daughter of being gay and having a relationship with my foster child. (I believe no one should ever be shamed. His accusations were false; she is only fourteen and she isn't even interested in dating right now.)

The drama came about because my father saw my daughter and foster child watching a scene on the TV show *Riverdale* where two girls were making out in the hallway. He completely overre-acted and started messaging my friends on Facebook, asking them how they feel about me allowing my fourteen-year-old daughter to watch two girls together. I thought, *Uhhhh, no, I am not going to make them change the channel because it is just as natural for two girls to kiss as it is for a man and a woman to kiss.* He later said he acted that way because he was jealous that they were spending so much time together. What!?!

Soooooo, I started setting my boundaries once it started affecting my children. I don't always know how to set boundaries for myself, but let someone mess with my children and an old mama bear comes out roaring, ready to defend them! I don't stand up for myself like I should, but I am so quick to defend my kids, which most of the time also ends up protecting me.

I will never forget what my father did. And I am learning to slowly set boundaries for myself and my family. I don't know where his sense of entitlement comes from, but at one point during the drama, he even told me and my husband that he will gladly leave when we pay for him to go to a nursing home.

At the time of writing this book, the housing market is crazy! There is more demand than there are available homes. We spent a long time looking for our next place to call home. With a pandemic among us, the kids still in virtual learning, and Tim and I still working from home mostly, we decided that we needed a bigger home, so we built a new home. We are in the process of moving into the home we have patiently been waiting for over a year. We sold our previous home in January and lived in an RV on a military installation for nine weeks. To say it feels good to be into a home that we designed is an understatement.

While my father did not move with us, I didn't leave him homeless, either. We helped him find a place and aided in a smooth transition. I found a room for him to rent where he has three roommates, all men around his age, and it seems to be working well. Thank the Lordt! One of his roommates is a chef. They feed him and everything! If that isn't a Higher Being at work, I don't know what is! And we are working on rekindling our relationship. Even my kids, in particular my youngest, Bernie, enjoys his nightly phone conversations with him. It's lovely. He comes, helps out and hangs out, then goes back to his place. I couldn't have asked for a better situation. All I know is that my home will always be a space of love and peace for my children to always come home to. No one will take that from us.

<u>**Fatherhood**</u>
After 20 years, he's back in my life.
Oh, how the young me has cried and cried.
But as I got older and had to survive,
What a warrior I've become.

He thought leaving was best somehow.
At the time, it didn't feel that way,
But now I can say his DNA,
His genetic code didn't make me.
I did.

I don't have any emotion either way.
I've grown numb to the pain,
Calloused at the mention of him
He set the precedence for what I would take
From any man who entered my life
After he left.

But now that he's back,
He did have the chance to walk me down the aisle
And hand me over to a deserving man,
Who chose responsibility of family over freedom,
The real example my children will see.

It may be too late for us to connect;
He is a stranger to me.
But I do respect his opportunity
To bond with his grandkids.
After all, they are innocent.

Let's see how he handles another attempt

At a reciprocating family.
A give and take—not take and take.
I am awake,
I am on guard.
I will protect, and I will discard
At the very instant he tries to hurt
Anyone here that he has already deserted once.
Pain has no place here.

I don't know if I am at a place of healing yet, but I am still and will always be at the place of protection. Because the trauma of him leaving at such an early age caused a lot of my life choices, the act of him coming back allowed me to face my choices. For many, it might not take a physical presence of standing face to face with your past for closure, but I acknowledge that for me, it did. Some may be able to just accept things for what they are and work internally to get through it. I'm not sure I would have ever been able to internally work through it if he hadn't physically come back into my life.

I love my mother, but I have even had to set some boundaries with her. She probably won't admit this, but she is a hoarder. I think that played a role in her decision to not move to Virginia. We wanted her to get rid of some of her stuff. There was no space for it here.

I remember one time the sewer system in Johnstown was failing everywhere, so the city made every household replace pipes from the house to the road. We paid for that for her, but first, her basement flooded with all kinds of sewer water. It was disgusting. And even then she didn't want to part with the stuff in the basement that was covered in poop water.

I also think that plays a role in why we don't visit there as often as I want to. There's nowhere for us to really be in her home. The fact that she has stuff everywhere makes me feel awful. I know she works a lot and was taking care of my older brother. And now, she is dealing with the sadness of having to put him in a home. He had some medical issues come up and had been violent with her. This was the only choice. And it is weighing on her.

I get it. Life gets hard sometimes. I help as much as I can. And when I can't, I have learned I have to say "no" sometimes. I have learned there are other ways I can help. I hate saying no, but I can't do everything. That is life, and I am learning to live with that.

There have been other times when I have had to learn to set boundaries. When we lived in Beaverdam, we lived close to Kings Dominion. I worked there, and we all had season passes. This was one of the best times of my life! Life is good at amusement parks!

During our time in Beaverdam, I also worked at a flooring company where I handled sales and took on interviewing potential employees. I hired a fascinating woman, whom I ended up adopting as my second mama. I am a firm believer that we don't have to confine our family to biology. We can pick and choose our family and can decide if people are no good for our lives, even if they have relation to us.

She and I had an instant connection. She moved into our guest home and did everything with us, even joining us for our weekly trips to Kings Dominion. I am sure my mom didn't like someone else coming in and taking on this role to her grandkids, and I am pretty sure my father didn't care for it either, but at this time in my life, it was nice to have someone here.

We discussed intricate plans to build a bed and breakfast with a bakery in it. She would run the bakery, and I would manage the bed and breakfast portion. She was an amazing pastry chef. We spent years looking at land, homes, businesses, and probably every piece of property for sale in Virginia.

Sadly, once we decided that we needed to sell that home and move so my husband could be closer to his work, she found a home in the Northern Neck with a relative. We stayed in an apartment until we found our home. Even though I was raised in the city, I quickly realized apartment living wasn't for me.

I never considered myself a country girl, but I was finding myself enjoying the quiet and privacy of country living. I felt safe surrounded by nature. Our next home was on even less land, just three acres. But it did have a guest apartment above the garage. This was nice because we were able to keep it empty when we wanted to use it for movie nights or as an office. But when we wanted to have extra cash, we rented it out.

At one point, my adopted mama had to leave the Northern Neck because she was having a hard time and also had to shut her business down, so she went to live with her boyfriend. Soon after, she was struggling there and had to leave, so we invited her back in, but our relationship was never the same.

Her dog was getting older and was unable to go up and down the steps of the garage apartment. Inside, our home was somewhat small and tight. She tried sharing a room with my daughter, but that was on the second floor, and her dog fell down our steps. We bought a small RV to try to make that work but she wasn't happy because she had to come inside to use the bathroom until we could get it connected to the septic.

We started finding out she was going behind our back with the kids and trying to stir trouble, especially with the foster children. She was starting to tell me things that they were doing, and then tell them I said things I wasn't saying. Luckily, my children would come to me and show me what she was saying. She was trying to cause issues between my husband and me also.

One time, there was a foster care party, and we didn't bring her with us. I guess my youngest son, who was very young at the time, told her she didn't belong at this party, and that turned weird. She went to every kid, asking them if I was talking about her, saying my son, Bernie, wouldn't have said that if I wasn't. She returned to a time in her life where she was told she didn't belong, and it seemed like she had some sort of meltdown. But this persisted.

I later found out she was buying drugs from people both of my foster children knew. I believe her change in behavior was caused by drug use. She started getting a little scary at the end. She would barge into my home, yelling at me. She got paranoid and would hear the voice of God, using that as a reason to do, or not do, certain things. She started acting very differently. I eventually had to ask her to leave.

Start Anew
I don't understand what led to the end.
You came to us as family and friend
And left as someone else, in fact a stranger.
I loved you, but
My need to protect my children was greater

Things were great until we had to sell our home.
I realize that was a hardship for you,
And it led to a tough time for you, I know.
But even when you moved, you were still family,
And you moved in with someone you loved from your ancestry

Then, something happened there, and you had to go
I cared, and I invited you in...but I know
It wasn't ideal for you. I didn't have the space,

And I tried to work with what I had
So that you wouldn't be displaced.

I did the best I could. I bought an RV
I know it wasn't how you wanted life to be,
But it was only temporary until we figured something else out,
Until I found out things were going on behind my back,
Conniving with my children, I had to react

My whole purpose in life is to love and protect my kids,
So I did what I had to do. And I asked you to leave.
I felt so deceived.
And that day in the courtroom, I didn't even know you.
You called me names under your breath.
You had so much hate inside you.
It wasn't right, and throughout that time of my life
I just wanted to help you...and love you...

It has now been a couple years since we have
seen or heard from you.
I often wonder where you are
And how you are
And wish I had more time with you.
I really hope life is being good to you.

The time you were here was probably the best in my life.
The adventures we had,
The connections we shared,
I'll keep it in my memories.
And if you ever stumble this way again,
I'm sure we can mend and rebuild
And start anew

Because that's what friends and family do

After I asked her to leave, it didn't happen quickly. I gave her time to find some place, but as she looked, it was getting increasingly difficult to be on the same property with her. She would come into my house and yell at me. I eventually had to go to the court system and ask that she be removed. She left willingly and had some people come help her move her belongings. She even took a shit in the RV that never got connected to the septic on her way out.

There was a court hearing, and she still showed up even though she had already moved out. It sounded like she was trying to tell the judge that she was my nanny and deserved to stay, but the judge told her that it was my property, and since I asked her to leave, she had to oblige.

As she was leaving the courthouse, she was angry and threatened me under her breath. The combination of those threats mixed with the things she said to the judge prompted the sheriff to ask me to stay in the courtroom for about ten minutes. He wanted to ensure she was gone before I went to my car. They sensed there might be trouble. Oddly, a few minutes later she came barging back into the courtroom, muttering more hate under her breath. I didn't wait. I just ran to my car, and that was the last time I saw her.

I am sad about it, but I had to protect my family. I will always care for her, and I don't have ill feelings towards her. Apparently, she was only meant to be in our lives for a little while, and the next part of my journey wasn't meant to be walked with her alongside me. Not everyone is meant to stay with us in each season of our lives. God has it all worked out ahead of time, and I will not fret.

So here we are, living the life. New home. New life. And what a transition! We moved to a waterfront community and feel that this is all a part of my healing process. I find peace in the water. In fact, one of my life songs is called "Oceans (Where Feet May Fail)" by Hillsong UNITED. You can breathe it in at https://www.youtube.com/watch?v=dy9nwe9_xzw.

I believe in the power of music. This song is about being called out into the water, or anything in life that is unknown and mysterious, but having the faith to walk on water. And even when we are in the deep waters, this is when we are in His embrace, and His grace embraces us. Just let the Spirit lead you. Read Matthew 14:22-32 to read about Peter, walking on water with doubt in the storm. He was between the safety of the boat and the safety of Jesus when Jesus told him to come to Him. He saw the wind, got scared, and began to sink. He asked Jesus to save him, and He did. I like to find songs that speak to my soul.

And boy does this song shout at me!

Being a giver is really hard for me. I used to give until I had nothing left to give. And even then, I would try to find something of myself to give. It's destructive sometimes and something I have to work very hard at. It's strange to have some of the issues I struggle with. How can I have a hard time spending money and have issues with money hoarding but at the same time give it all away? I grew up not having money, so when I do have it, I want to keep it all. But let someone come to me in need and those worries go away. I will give everything. Crazy, right? But I have found that because I have a giving heart, I am rarely in need. I receive bountifully so that I can help the next person.

I have a hard time saying no. I have always been this way. So I had to create a catchphrase for my NO in order to feel power over these times when I needed to say no. My go-to phrase is: "Unfortunately, I can't." It was so hard to come up with that even though it is such a simple thing to say. I used to make it long and drawn out, full of excuses. But I have learned to just say, "Unfortunately, I can't," and then shut up. If they ask why, I will give a short, valid reason like "I can't fit it into my schedule," or sometimes I blame it on my husband and say, "My husband would kill me if I said yes."

I have learned to be reliable for myself, and when times get hard, I turn to myself. The hard part is that a part of me is giving pieces of me to others. I am me when I am helping those around me. I took a lot of time to get to know myself, and I realized that the things I love about me, others will also find useful. There have surely been some times when I had nothing to give, and those were probably my lowest times. But once I accepted my journey as having to happen in order to help someone else at a later time, it brought peace to me even through the hard times. The more I can help someone else, the more I feel like I am living life. So having to create boundaries around the ways in which I am able to give without taking away from myself or those I love was very hard, but necessary. This is me. I have to set boundaries for myself over and over again.

Self-Reflection:

1. Are there times in your life you felt guarded? What situations in your life prompted you to feel this way? It's amazing to feel protective of yourself. That is a part of self-care. What things did you do to guard yourself? How did you feel when defending yourself against those who hurt or took advantage of you? What have you learned about yourself in the process of setting boundaries for yourself? List some boundaries that you have been able to set for yourself in the space below.

____

____

____

____

____

2. Are there people in your life who you are constantly on guard around? Perhaps you should evaluate those relationships. Not everyone in your life right now is meant to walk with you during your entire journey of life. Free yourself from people who pull you down. For me, I had to physically remove them from my space in order to feel free from them. List some ways here in which you can free yourself from those who hurt you and bring you down.

____

____

____

____

____

3. What is something you would be comfortable saying when telling someone no? Once you come up with it, call two close friends and tell them your go-to-phrase. How did they react?

____

____

____

____

____

chapter 9

LIVING IN A WORLD THAT'S CRUMBLING

I am writing this book in the midst of a pandemic. COVID-19 has hit the world and has taken over the lives of many. Small businesses are shutting down. Restaurants are closing. We have had to change so much of how we live our day-to-day lives.

We Doordash (a food delivery service) when we don't feel like cooking. We Amazon shop or get groceries delivered. We drive and hang out only with those who live in our household. We don't travel by public transportation. We celebrate through virtual parties and hold virtual meetings instead of going into the office. The elderly are dying alone. We wear masks everywhere we go. We avoid people. Many have lost their jobs. At the time of publication, we have been at this for over two years now. While some places are starting to open up, and those who received the vaccine are now allowed to go without a mask in some locations, we are nowhere near what we used to be prior to the pandemic. It's sad.

We are in a constant cycle of shutting down and cautiously opening back up, trying to get this pandemic under control.

For two school years, my children have been doing virtual

learning. I don't know what the future holds for their education. They aren't hanging out with friends or going out in public. They wake up at 8:29 a.m. when they have to be on the computer in class at 8:30 a.m. They get their answers from Alexa, the Amazon virtual assistant. They are eating, listening to music, and playing on their phones when they should be paying attention.

My husband and I have both been working from home. At the time of writing this book, he is fully vaccinated and has started traveling for work again. I also reluctantly got vaccinated when I was considering applying for a job, as it has become mandatory for some employees to be fully vaccinated in order to work.

We used to travel all the time. The year before the pandemic hit, we took our first family plane ride to New Orleans to get on a cruise where we visited Mexico, the Cayman Islands and Jamaica. It was amazing, and I love that my kids are getting older and we can enjoy time together. Since the pandemic occurred, we haven't traveled anywhere where we could enjoy time with other people.

For the past two years, we have pretty much been confined to the four walls of our home. We go on nature walks and on boat rides to places we know we wouldn't be around many people. But the majority of our time has been spent inside. In the summer of 2021, I did take a driving trip with the kids to Georgia for an isolated beach trip and Florida for another beach trip, which was awful. Red tide hit the entire area, so the beaches were covered in dead fish and dead birds. It smelled awful, and people were getting sick from this algae, including my son, Bernie. I was so worried we weren't going to be able to get back home because they may have mistaken his red tide sickness with COVID-19.

Now that the pandemic is ending, I am really looking forward to more trips with them. Time is running out. My oldest is seventeen now and will be an adult soon. Who knows what kind of change that will bring...

Our previous home was beautiful; it just wasn't big enough. We had to put a lot of work into it to make it what it was. After moving in, we learned that the previous owner built the garage with an apartment above it and never closed the permit, even after turning in drawings of a garage with storage above. We were left responsible for the tons of work the previous owner left for us, including an underground leak that we couldn't get under control, installing a whole new drain field to accommodate the extra apartment, fixing a roof leak, which required us to replace the roof, replacing the HVAC when it stopped working, and the well pump, which went bad. It was one issue after another.

Because we put so much work into that home, we decided to add on another bathroom and a dining room. That ended up taking over a year and a half, however...deep into COVID-19. Six months in, we were looking around at houses and found the most beautiful subdivision. We didn't hesitate. We put a down payment on a new construction home and started designing.

This turned out to be the best decision we could have made. Not only did we come in with instant equity because of how crazy the market is right now, the new home is bigger and has more private space for us and the kids. I have an office to work from home. And while the lot is smaller than our last home, we have community land that we can use. Just a block from our new home are ponds to fish in, a playground, boat ramps to the James River, a swimming pool, trails, and a gym. It's nice for the kids to be able to safely get out of the house and have fun. Maybe even meet new friends! We moved from a very busy road and were stuck on our property unless we got into the car and drove somewhere.

I was tired of feeling stuck.

Even though it didn't seem like it at the time, the entire process happened in the way it was supposed to. We ended up selling our home in January 2022. We were supposed to be in the new home in February, so we sold everything and bought an RV. We lived on a military installation for a total of nine weeks with my husband and me, our three kids, two dogs, and three cats. Much longer than anticipated, but there were hold-ups with the new home, mainly with building materials and contractors.

Remodeling and moving is a good metaphor for what is going on in the world today. Pandemic aside, a bigger issue consuming the world around us is hate and racism—and so much of it. My daughter is Black. The forces lined up in such a way that we had a Black president who left office in 2016 followed by a president who brought forth many bad things like racism and white supremacy. During 2020 through 2022, some people have come out of the hills to demonstrate their hate towards people different from them, including Black people and LGBTQ+ people.

In fact, 2021 was an election year, and the incumbent president didn't win, so his followers stormed the Capitol to try to change the results of the election while doing a lot of damage and destruction. Lives were lost that day.

In Virginia where I live, and in other areas of the United States, local statues are being taken down that represent racism and hatred. This has caused more divide. Some say these statues are a representation of Southern pride. In Richmond, some people say that you can't have Monument Avenue without monuments. Others say we don't need such hateful statues in the streets where our children play. They say these statues would be better in a museum. Either way, change is coming, and it starts in the hearts. We can change street names and take down statues all day long, but if the people aren't ready to receive it, there will be trouble.

<u>Statues Crumbling</u>
The statues they are crumbling,
The statues they are coming down.
Erected to intimidate,
Standing tall to draw them out.
No one wanted to integrate
The statues stand to perpetuate hate…

But today, the statue is coming down.
History is being made,
Moving in the right direction,
Honoring the lives lost in the name of hate
Future is being changed,
A better life for those to come
A small battle won…

Our kids may now see sunny days,
The view now clear, statue not in the way.
The statues they are crumbling.
We see hate all around,
People mad at freedom found.
We also see good people stand,
Pushing for equality,
Embarking in an uprising
That starts with the crumbling…

This is just the beginning,
The start to bringing unity.
Hand in hand, we march and fight
In the cause of what is right
They are coming down so you can rise,
Take back your life, move onward, fight!

We all unite to change the world,
Drown out hate. So little Black boys and little Black girls
Have a chance at life.
Chanting, "Black lives matter" until they do.
The statues are crumbling so this can be true
People are hurting, but this is the beginning
Of an undeniable uprising.
History is taking place in front of me
While the statues are crumbling...

The rebel flag, a sign of hate,
Designed to continue segregate
Fear instilled in the hearts of some
But the statues crumbling, a small justice won
Those against it, complaining and shaming
All kinds of blaming...

How could we want to erase history, they say—
As if taking the statue from public view will somehow
Take the past away.

That's not the point, the streets are not the place
To embrace the displays of such hate...
Too much pain to see every day.
Take them away!

Then name each victim and say it loud,
Shout it out to the crowd,
Chanting as they are crumbling.
Anger can eventually turn to healing...
Step by step small battles won,
Hands up, guns down...

In kneeling, we see victory,
Let's leave hate in the history,
Continue peaceful combat for
A world that's free...unity...
until we win the whole damn war—
fighting for equality...

In my opinion, those statues being removed in Richmond and other areas mean nothing and shouldn't be a cause for such a divide. I urge you to take time and listen to the other side. Listen when they tell you it causes them pain. Listen when they tell you that all they want to do is move forward. We owe every person we encounter the opportunity to hear them out. It's not a huge gesture to show we are not at that place anymore. We truly do have the power to all break bread together and get through this.

I'll be the first to admit that not that long ago, I had a hard time recognizing some of these things as hate. I am from Pennsylvania and didn't quite understand that hate ran so deep against the Confederate "rebel" flag. It took me sitting down with different people and hearing their position to understand where they were coming from. Hearing how some older local neighbors dealt with slurs thrown at them, getting their houses vandalized while someone threw a burning Confederate flag on their property. And all kinds of ish. It took me hearing their stories and the lives they have lived to understand their pain. And ultimately, we as a society should avoid singling a whole group of people out. We should want to stand up when someone else is being held down. It is our humanity.

Currently, there is another crisis going on around us. People fleeing other countries, like Haiti and Afghanistan. Immigrants and refugees are coming to America in monumental numbers. Some in America have hate towards the newcomers, saying negative things, screaming at them to go back to their countries, and wondering why we spend so many resources on others when we have so many hurting in our country.

The LGBTQ+ community has also been targeted for far too long, and it really bothers my soul. Some people try to use religion or politics to stand against them, but this isn't human decency.

I hate to think this kind of racism, prejudice, and hate is still occurring because we now have a Black, female vice president, but I am so proud that my daughter gets to witness this monumental change going on in America right now. To me, it doesn't matter who the president is because we the people have the power to change the world! Every single one of us. We can do more together than apart. In 2022, we are at a better place than we were last year. It feels like we are rebuilding in a way. It seems the hearts and eyes of many Americans are being opened, and I have slowly seen change come over us.

Matthew 8:20 says that Jesus replied, "Foxes have dens and birds have nests, but the Son of Man has no place to lay His head." According to this Bible verse, Jesus was a refugee. He came to earth with nothing. No home, nowhere to lay, fleeing the slaughter of all innocent children under the age of two. Jesus taught us to always reach out to those in need, even the refugee and the immigrant. Could you imagine if Jesus was among us during this refugee crisis we are facing today?

LGBTQ+ LOVE

Gender-free or gender-less,
Clothed in a suit or in a dress,
Masculine or feminine,
Testosterone or estrogen,
Genderblind, love everyone,

Not caring to be in a relationship at all,
Transgender or questioning,
Genes, chromosomes, genitals,
Who fucking cares?
For. Real.

But but but...it's not very Christian-like
Who says?
Is that your interpretation?
That's what's wrong with this nation.
Forcing our neighbor to live in isolation
Because of our blind and sometimes blatant discrimination.
But scripture says—

What does it say?
Don't take an isolated passage
And hold it hostage
Study the entire topic
And you will see
We are losing our humanity.

Jesus' only command was LOVE.
Love thy neighbor.
Instead, gender diversity
Is facing hate from the masses.
What asses are we!

Take away their rights in the name of religion and politics,
Choose a political party with less government.
What you mean is,
you don't want to be controlled;
You want to be in control of those not like you.

If our LGBTQ+ community can't be legally protected,
Then we must step in.
It is our duty as allies
To do what the government is failing at.
They shall no longer be denied based on their identities.
No more exclusion, demand equality.
Stop the oppression, end the injustice.
Give them a reason to trust us.

Wait wait wait—but marriage is between
A bride and the church,
A man and a woman,
There's no other option.
Anything else is not a part of the masterplan.
But I would argue this is certainly not true.
Yes, God made woman and man,
But the Bible doesn't say He only had
A BINARY plan.

You will see in the very few scriptures
That addresses homosexuality
God isn't speaking of a loving committed relationship
He is speaking to you and me.
He is speaking to our hearts.
All this HATE isn't the heart of God
But the heart of man.
He's speaking to our morality.
Through the lessons in His Word.

In these few verses, He is addressing
Sexual violence, laying with young boys, molesting.
He addresses continuing our lineage

Yet eunuchs existed in Bible times.
So, to say marriage is exclusively between a man and a woman
Just because others weren't addressed
Is intolerant.
Stop the resistance.

At the end of our lives,
God looks at our souls.
Our body is made from dust.
It won't be coming with us in the afterlife.
Our body is the keeper of our souls
As we roam this earth
But our biology won't be coming with us.
Our body will pass away and return to dust.

So please, try not to be so disgusting
In your hate for the soul of our neighbors.
Jesus looks at the heart.
Not at genitals, not at skin, not even at my potty mouth.
So, in this day in history,
Let us celebrate the victory
Of gender equality
As we show love to our LGBTQ+ community.

Our children are watching
Let's demonstrate a liberating love
To humankind.
And honor justice
Exalted in unity.
We fellowship with other souls
For a better world and a better life lived.

I get irritated with people who use Bible verses to justify being straight-up hateful to people in the LGBTQ+ community. It's easy to pick one sentence in the Bible and make it mean anything you want it to mean, but to be genuine, you have to take context, translation, and even interpretation into consideration. In fact, an amazing pastor I know told me a lot of today's Bibles in English haven't been translated correctly and have been changed to say what the translator wanted it to say.

Yeah, I said it.

Being against the LGBTQ+ community fits some people's narratives, so they spread the hate instead of the LOVE shown all throughout the Bible. In the very few instances where it talks about a man lying with a man, either they are talking about pagan orgies worshipping other gods, child molestation, gang rape, cheating on your wife with another male, etc. Nothing is said about loving, committed same-sex relationships. So how can we say gay marriage is an abomination?

You know what is also an abomination according to the Bible? Sleeping with your wife while she is menstruating. How many times do you see people protesting that? You can't cut your beard or wear silk and polyester blend clothing, either according to the Old Testament, but we are somehow okay with that, too. This is why context is everything.

The Bible talks about eunuchs, people who don't procreate by choice, by force (castration) or by birth. And also, marriage back then was so different than it is now. We can't even compare. If a girl is raped, sold, moved in with a man, accidentally sleep with the wrong person in a tent, or a father gives consent, according to the Bible, they are married. So all this "marriage is between man and woman" and "between Adam and Eve, not Adam and Steve" or whatever people try to say, it is insensitive. The Bible is very clear about how we should treat people and how important it is to love. I believe these were a couple of verses on same-sex sex written during a time when it was the norm to have a little "side meat," but nothing that is directed against same-sex marriage.

Marriage is weird, anyway. I read this meme that totally resonated with me. It said, "Whoever invented marriage was creepy as hell. Like, I love you so much I'm gonna get the government involved so you can't leave."

I felt that.

Jesus knew we have trouble with discrimination, which is why he emphasized the story of the good Samaritan. For context, you can read Luke 10: 27-37. A man was attacked by robbers, beaten, stripped, and left for dead on the side of the road. A Jewish Priest and a Levite walked by and crossed the road to avoid him. But a Samaritan (even though Samaritans and Jewish people hated each other) helped him. He took care of his wounds and took him to an inn to care for him. How is that for love thy neighbor?

I genuinely believe if Jesus was here, He would scoff at the way people are treated. I know throughout history that there have always been laws in place that were not always in the best interest of the citizens, like death to adulterers or the disobedient who were exiled. Prison was not really a sentence in Bible times. It was just a place of confinement and torture until judgement. And I'm not sure a whole lot has changed since then in regards to law and order.

I believe in a system of unitive and restorative justice, not punitive justice. A system where someone has the ability to grow and to heal, not just be punished for what they have done. A system of love, not revenge. A structure of compassion and sincere oneness with those around us. We have evolved and need more community and opportunities to restore humanity. We are no longer primitive beings that must resort to hurt and violence to make a point. As I have demonstrated throughout my life, sometimes I have done stupid shit out of survival, but my heart is good. Could you imagine if stones were thrown at me for the mistakes I have made, eliminating the chance for me to be restored into making a difference in this world?

The government influences society by putting laws in place, and these laws are used as political tools. I have a hard time when the government is sworn to serve and protect, yet then fights to create laws, and therefore punishments, for people considered outcasts. But then they use religion as the basis, even though there is supposed to be a separation of the church and state. Same-sex marriage bans, laws against interracial marriage, abortion laws...many laws have been in place throughout time, and good citizens fight every day for justice and for basic human rights.

Don't get me wrong, we have come a long way. For instance, in the real estate world, here in Virginia we have recently added to our protected class through our fair housing laws to include sexual orientation, gender identity, veteran status, and source of income. It is now illegal to discriminate when buying, selling, renting, etc. in regards to race, color, religion, national origin, sex, elderliness, familial status, disability, source of funds, sexual orientation, gender identity, and veteran status. Seeing as I feel home ownership should be attainable by all, this means a lot to me. At the end of the day, my life passion lies in loving and accepting all while trying to bridge a gap in society against those who have been deserted and abandoned in the public eye.

When we are called to "love thy neighbor," this doesn't mean to just love those who look like us or talk like us. The world is our neighbor. We are not to judge anyone. The things clear as day in the Bible are, love thy neighbor and be His hands and feet. Everything else is pish-posh, so why dwell on it and why make enemies by trying to tell someone else how to live when they don't agree with you? That is all that matters. Love thy neighbor. **The world is our neighbor.**

At the end of the day, we are a spirit. When we leave this earth, this physical body we carry around will not go with us. This means my vagina doesn't make me who I am so why do we feel we need to dictate if someone should or shouldn't be able to fall in love with another person with a vagina? The reality is that a person's soul is pretty special, and that is where the connection lies. When we pass, our genitals, our skin color, and any of that shit that causes hate and division—none of it will go with us! So why do we focus so heavily on it?

To me, there is a joyfulness in connecting with spiritual beings. It is uplifting to think about all of the good we can do if we work together and live by the golden rule. In Jesus' short life, the only commandment He ever gave us was to love thy neighbor. That's it!! And I live by that every day. It's so fulfilling...

Life doesn't have to be so hard. We make it that way. And when you take COVID-19 and hate and mix it together, you get a war going on all around in so many different directions. It's a scary time for so many right now.

Fight from all Directions

In a world that's cold and struck by a plague,
A contagion of hate, an infection of rage,
Fallen on hard times, COVID-19
Job loss, death, losing everything.

On top of this virus, a war on race emerges...
What little progress we've ever made
Has now started reversing.
We find closeness in riots in the street,

But isolation in the home.
It's a sad, sad world, we are all on our own...

The government has abandoned us.
We are turning on each other.
Can we not see that
We will only get through this together?

If only we could know that love is the answer
Instead of fleeing towards hate that's eating us like cancer...
It's not just a local dilemma, it's gone viral!
The world has joined in—
humanity depends on global unity for survival...

Right now, we are facing numerous threats to our existence,
And the only way to have a chance is to take a stance,
Join together, care for each other...
Love your neighbor, your sister, and your brother.

Through the pandemic and race war,
Love has got to be the cure.
Stand together and fight through the conflict,
Or the human race will become extinct.

With people dying from this disease
And people dying in the streets,
Death doesn't just knock at the door of the frail and weak.
We are all at the mercy of something higher than we.
Speak for the weak, the lonely, and the sick,
Stand up for the powerless, the poor, the unguarded, the addict.

We are all in this together, can't run, can't hide...

The impact is hitting populations worldwide...
Fight for each other, stand hand in hand,
Don't let hate win, spread love as fast as we can.

Spend every day radiating kindness, dispersing hope,
Fostering goodness in hearts around the globe...
Be generous intentionally, make choices for peace.
Bring the world to their knees...

Kneel for inequality, for suffering and oppression...
We must stand together and continue progression...
Keep moving forward in humanity
Value life systematically.

If we can't get it together for all of humankind,
Make room in our hearts and open our minds,
Build relationships and human connections,
We could lose this fight coming at us from all directions...

My entire hope for us is that we can somehow find common ground. We are all more alike than we think if we just take the time to listen and love one another. We have the power to get through this and end up stronger than ever before. I recognize that I am gifted the armor of white skin in this sometimes racist world. So I use my white voice when I need it to help anyone in trouble.

<u>Save Humanity</u>
The color of humanity.
I'm clothed in my armor of white skin,
Bore in the house I was birthed in
I didn't choose it but I'm protected.

Rarely suspected, mostly respected.
Solely based on the covering of my blood.
Yet we All. Bleed. Red.

What were we thinking
When we thought it would ever be okay
To own a human being and treat them that way?
And the pain they encountered
Now passes down generations
As hate gravitates to the different races.
The plot thickens.

You're set up, convicted,
A crime not even committed.
Your child raised without you.
Can't afford a good home.
On a one-parent income.
Property tax determines school investments.
Who's there to invest in you?

No good education,
Generation after generation,
Broken people break people.
Your kids on the street
On welfare sucking the government tit.
Control over you and what you do.
How do you work up the chain
If you can't even obtain
Enough to get out of poverty?
And the vicious cycle continues.

How about a revolution?

Let's start with our children.
Our children who are born to love
Until someone teaches them not to.
Let's show them LOVE...
And regulate what they hear and see.
Protect them from society.

We can't turn back the hands of history,
But we can command our future.
Begin the change within ourselves,
Advance ahead, take precedence
In the change we demand to see.
Transform the way we view humanity.

We have the power to alter our future.
Let's celebrate our differences
And recognize our oneness.
Become connected
We have the ability to end racism
And save ourselves from the home-bred terrorism.

Stand united, for equality,
Equal opportunity.
Justice for all, and all, and all.
Tear down the wall dividing us.
It's treacherous.
If only we stand hand in hand, stand firm,
Affirm unity with our individual identities,
Associating with our character, abilities,
Our accreditation,
Not by our complexion.
Not by our skin.

Only then can the campaign begin
If enough of us resist
And fight the battle to coexist
In love.

Another crisis going on all around the globe is human trafficking and the poor treatment of females in general. There was recently an investigation going on about a woman from New York who went on a road trip with her boyfriend. She went missing and he came home without her. Days later, they found her body. Watching this really hit me hard. I couldn't help but sit there and cry for her. And later, they found him too. He died by suicide, taking the easy way out.

There were so many signs in this case. Men take women far away from the people they know so they have no one and make them totally reliant. Then, they hit you for the first time over a jealous rage, but soon after, they act like it was because they love you so much they can't bear the thought of another man looking at you. They bring you flowers and smother you with gifts only to continue to slowly show more control and more aggression.

It's a roller coaster— women can't escape if they have no job, no money, no vehicle, and no friends. They are alone with no one to turn to. It isn't an overnight transformation. It is a long, drawn-out plan of diminishing your self-worth and taking over. By the time you realize you are in an abusive relationship, it is too late and too hard to even wrap your mind around how you will get out. A trauma bond is formed by repeating this cycle of abuse, making you feel bad, then showering you with gifts and affection or whatever you need.

Watching this case took me back and stopped my heart for a brief moment. This could have easily been me. I could have been the body found in the woods. So many women are going through this.

I wish I could hug every single one of them and tell them they deserve better. They deserve love. I don't have the most affectionate husband, but I am happy every single day of my life with him. And when I really need acts of love, he is there. I have to tell him, but he is there.

I get so saddened by the fight women have to endure in this world. How we have to be told to dress appropriately, to carry pepper spray, to not get drunk, and to cover our drinks when we are out. No one ever tells the man to leave us the hell alone.

I will have readers from all over the nation, so I will put the National Domestic Violence hotline number here; if you find yourself in a situation, and you need help, please seek help. Call 800-799-7233 for free, confidential, 24/7 help. Everyone deserves to feel safe and to be in a loving, healthy relationship, free from abuse.

It's tough being a woman. I am told all the time to be thankful I live in the United States because women in other countries have it a lot worse. The condition of the treatment of women in other countries doesn't negate the fact that women have a hard time here, too. We have laws created against us that tie our hands in saving our lives. No one wants to kill the babies when the topic of abortion comes up. We just want the right to protect our lives if something were to go wrong with the pregnancy. No one is pro-kill the babies; we are just pro-choice. We want to live. If a woman has to make that horrible decision, believe that there was no other choice.

At the time of writing this, there is a war on women. The Supreme Court has just voted to overturn Roe vs. Wade. Many states are creating new laws banning abortions. Some are strict, some are subtle, but this very decision is changing the lives of many women all over the country. Women are fearing for their lives and feeling like second class citizens. We are worried about what the future holds for us and our need for body autonomy. Thankfully this didn't happen a few years ago and I was able to get the care I needed, but I fear for the world my daughter has to live in.

Instead of creating laws to ban abortions, how about we focus on the before and after issues? In my opinion, we should help with more contraception assistance and sex education beforehand so we don't have to use abortion as a birth control plan. And shouldn't we have better plans in place to care for a baby after being born from parents who don't have the means to care for it? We should step up for humanity.

I am a firm believer in community. We are responsible for helping those around us. If we all took on that role, we wouldn't need to rely so heavily on government programs to take care of our people. We are to bear that responsibility. Life matters.

All life...

Black lives, women's lives, LGBTQ+ lives...those affected by wars, pandemics. There's so much hate and divide.

So how do we live in a world that has been crumbling? Maybe the world has to crumble just a little in order to build back up again. It may seem like chaos right now, but one day, we will wake up and the sun will be shining, and all kinds of people will be laughing and working together. Black people, white people, gay people, and straight people. Women, men, people vaccinated, and people wearing masks. We will all coexist in love for life and humanity. How nice that will be.

Self-Reflection:

1. This can be a scary world sometimes. Do you have any memory of things that happened in your life and the world around you that has scared you or even crippled you in fear?

____

____

____

____

____

2. How did you get through your fear? Always think small and work your way out. What affirmations can you tell yourself in times of fear? Write these down. Our thoughts are more powerful than we can imagine. Just telling ourselves a statement of affirmation can get us through some pretty tough times.

____

____

____

____

____

3. Once you have calmed your thoughts, is there a space in your home you can go to that makes you feel safe, even if you might not live in an area that you feel safe in? If you can't control the big, focus on controlling the small spaces around you. Choose a space, maybe a closet or a specific room, and decorate it in a way that makes you feel safe and protected. Some people use candles, lights, scents, play music, and some put art on the wall. Maybe a prayer rug. Make it a space that allows you to connect with yourself. A place where you feel relaxed. Write about this place and how you will connect with it in the space provided.

____

____

____

____

____

____

4. Now, how can you relate to someone who may also feel fear? How can you connect with someone going through something scary, and how can you help them get through it? Maybe someone you know is being assaulted at home. Or maybe someone is being bullied for the way they look. We are all connected. The more we can help each other through hard times, the softer the world will be. Commit to listening to someone's story and try to relate to them and feel empathy for them.

———————————————————————————

———————————————————————————

———————————————————————————

———————————————————————————

———————————————————————————

5. What are some Bible verses that have helped get you through some hard times? I would love it if you could send them to me at commahappyenjoythepause@gmail.com. It may also help to put your favorite verses on a card and carry it with you to remind you that you are never alone. The universe is always in your favor.

———————————————————————————

———————————————————————————

———————————————————————————

———————————————————————————

———————————————————————————

———————————————————————————

self-induction

chapter 10

THOU SHALT RECOGNIZE THE GOOD PEOPLE, EVEN IN A CRUMBLING WORLD

Fred Rogers once said, "When I was a boy, and I would see scary things in the news, my mother would say to me, 'Look for the helpers. You will always find people who are helping.' So that is what I do." If you look for good, you will find good.

Bad things in life are inevitable. They happen to the best of us —war. Disease. Murder. Illness. Viruses. Theft. We have all lost someone close to us who didn't deserve to leave this earth so early. We have all experienced something bad in our lifetimes. But in every instance of something bad happening, there is always good that follows. Sometimes, you really have to look for it, but it is there.

And while I fully believe in the concept of karma—good and bad—I still believe there is a lot in life that is left to chance. But I also believe this "chance" is really managed by a higher being, God, if you will. I believe that we have fate over different pieces of our destiny. If we put good out into the ether, we will receive good in return. If we have a bad spirit, we will feel wrath from it. But the path of a tornado, a moving cloud of torrential rains causing floods, the strike of lightning, a bear crossing our path, the joy of a rainbow, a hug at just the right moment, finding a $100 bill on the ground—all of these things seem like chance but they are guided by something bigger than us. And good people coming from all over the land to help in times of trouble is led by a guiding hand of comfort and shelter, arranged at just the right time, in just the right way by some higher being.

I can't recall a time when I was going through something hard and I had to face it on my own. There were always good people around, stepping in to do good. For instance, during one of the surrogacy pregnancies, my water broke very early. The baby was less than a viable age, and I had to spend a couple of months in the hospital on bed rest. While I was there, our whole community joined together to help my family. My husband and my kids had food delivered. People checked on us to make sure we were okay. I don't think my family could have gotten through this without the help of others.

I remember the tragic event of September 11, 2001, 9-11, when the planes crashed into the Twin Towers. There was death, destruction, and chaos that day. But I don't know if I recall a time when America was ever as joined together in solidarity as it was that day. Police and firefighters went in to save lives, volunteers did anything they could, offering food and water to those in need and those helping. People checked on their neighbors and loved ones. Pet rescues took place. There was so much love that came out of such a day of sorrow.

And as they say, if you can't find good in a situation, BE THE GOOD. Yes, the world needs helpers, and in order to have helpers, we need to BE the helpers.

St Teresa of Avila (1515-1582) wrote:

"Christ Has No Body

Christ has no body but yours,

No hands, no feet on earth but yours,

Yours are the eyes with which he looks

Compassion on this world,

Yours are the feet with which he walks to do good,

Yours are the hands, with which he blesses all the world.

Yours are the hands, yours are the feet,

Yours are the eyes, you are his body.

Christ has no body now but yours,

No hands, no feet on earth but yours,

Yours are the eyes with which he looks

compassion on this world.

Christ has no body now on earth but yours."

I genuinely believe that we are His hands and feet. We are put here to do good and to be good. We are here to be the helpers. According to Romans 12:6, we have different gifts, according to the graces given to each of us. Some serve, some give monetarily, and some heal. We all have a gift to use. Let's use them for the greater good!

Bad things are bound to happen within our lifetimes. And when they do, just look for the good people. And when we see something bad, we must step up and help those in need all around us. We must be the good.

When someone steps into my life in need, I receive at all the right times so that I can help them. My needs are always met so that I can continue to meet the needs of others. My favorite Bible verse that demonstrates this is 2 Corinthians 9:8, which says, "And God is able to bless you abundantly, so that in all things at all times, having all that you need, you will abound in every good work." I am always able to do what tugs at my heart in regards to helping others because I have been given so much.

A part of doing God's work is actually getting out there, doing it, and giving what we can give. We should use our crafts and our abilities to help when people are in need. When we give, we will be blessed to keep giving. We will always be provided for. In order to have a relationship with God, we must all have a good working relationship with each other and work together to help each other.

There have been many times in my life where I was in need and I was blessed at just the right time by just the right person. People in and out of my life have had a tug on their heart to help me, so they did and I was so blessed by it. The number one verse I live by is Romans 13: 8-9: "Let no debt remain outstanding, except the continuing debt to love one another, for whoever loves others has fulfilled the law. The commandments, "you shall not commit adultery," "you shall not murder," "you shall not steal," "you shall not covet," and all other commandments are summed up in this one command: ***"Love your neighbor as yourself."*** Just love.

It's a small world in the whole scheme of things. People will come in and out of our lives from the day we are born until the day of our death. Some stay longer than others, but we all serve a purpose in one another's lives. It's a big web of connections. They say there are six degrees of separation between every person that breathes on this earth. We are all just six introductions away from every person in existence. And the chances are that we have crossed paths with someone who may in one way or another help us or need our help in our future. That's a lot to grasp!

Once a person's purpose is fulfilled, we move on to the next purpose. Sometimes, a person walks into your life just to do good that one time, or to say that one thing to you, or to help you just once, and then, they go on to help the next person.

Not everyone will come with you through each season of your life. And that's okay. You will not walk with each person who enters your life through your entire time here on this earth. At times, someone's purpose is met, and then they walk away. Sometimes a person walking away had to be done in order to make your life better. And other times, them coming into your life made it better. The point is, treasure each moment, value the good around you, and appreciate when the moment must end to free yourself or others up in order to go on to the next purpose.

We may not always understand our purpose right now, but one day we will look back and think, *Wow! That's why I had to go through that!* John 13:7 says, "You do not realize now what I am doing, but later you will understand." And later, I ALWAYS understand.

Of course, I can say that my mother, my husband, my kids and the few friends I have are amazing people. After all, I don't let just anyone into my life. But sometimes, we are blessed with special people who are designed to remain with us throughout your life. I have someone in particular who has been such a blessing to my family and me. We met a pastor many years ago when we were living in Beaverdam, and he led the church we attended.

My pastor friend always gave sermons that agreed with my beliefs. He is spunky and full of life! He retired, we moved, and we attended several churches that didn't compare. One day, we attended a church and were thrilled to see him sitting in the back row! That church wasn't for me (because of a sermon given that said if we say an ugly four-letter word, it will lead us to hell. Here we go again with the threats!), but it led us to find out that soon after, he went to pastoring again at another church. We have seen him several times since. This church is a bit far from us, so we don't get there often, but I sure do check in with him as often as I can.

My pastor friend is the real deal, the true definition of servitude and compassion. I sought religion because I always thought it would help me. But I found out that I was spiritual without being engulfed with practicing religion. I'm getting good at being in tune with myself and those around me.

<u>The Love of God</u>

I'm not holier-than-thou,
I'm not religious,
I don't pass judgment.
Sometimes I cuss.
Okay, I cuss a lot...

I'm a spiritual being.
I don't like the institutions, the motions,
The rituals, the doctrines.
My faith comes from inside,
It's the experiences within.

The transformations,
In the minds and spirit.
Abstract...
Not needing an outward demonstration
Of practices and observations.

I'm one with nature,
I Reflect...meditate.
I don't feed into the politics,
The condemnations.

I seek inside myself for truth, for light, for life.

The LOVE of Jesus isn't found in ancient texts
By the interpretation of others.
It's found inside us.

LOVE unites, it doesn't divide.

I feel most connected to a higher being
When I am showing love and being loved.
The ultimate language.
Not out of fear.
Not thou shalt this—or thou shalt not that—
or you will go to hell.
NO!
Love doesn't do that.

I find coincidence in relating to some stories in the Bible,
But I realize it was written a long-ass time ago.
And can't possibly ALL apply to today. This day. In 2022.

I know God orchestrates the words in His Book,
Or words in a song,
Or words from a friend
At just the right time, right when I needed it.

I internalize that God is bigger than WE.
And fulfills our needs.
Jesus within, Jesus in me.
My hands and feet blessing others,
And their hands and feet blessing me.

It's all already arranged in a series of events.
Only God can do this.
In HIS time and HIS space.
That doesn't exist in the time of this life.
With Love.

I owe a lot of my inner peace to my pastor friend. I've learned so much from him and I go to him often. He is available to help all of the foster kids that come through my home.

Many of our foster children, and even my biological children, have reached out to him for help. For instance, one of our foster children was struggling with their gender identity. They struggled with whether they would be accepted in the church community, and they were worried about what an afterlife would look like for them. My pastor friend put them at ease by telling them a very close family member of his is transgender. He gave specific biblical instances to prove they are very much loved in the eyes of God, and it was really what they needed to hear.

He has offered counseling to children who have lost a parent. He relates to them and never makes them feel out of place or bad for the life they have endured. He comforts people in ways they need him and guides them through some serious shit sometimes. I'm not sure I could even take on the role of a foster parent if I didn't have him in my life. Hell, he has been here for me during some hard times I have endured over the years. He is an amazing human being.

I often vent to him about the foster care system as I do feel like we need reform. We need to focus more on helping families who need help and only removing children from their home as a last resort. It is very hard to be a foster parent. It is nice to be a foundation not just for the foster child but also their entire family. But I feel like the system has a lot of flaws, both for the biological parent who has their child ripped for them, and also for the foster parent who has their hands tied a lot of the time in regards to helping these children and doing what we see as best for them. It is a tough place to be, but I wouldn't want to be anywhere else right now.

<u>The System</u>
The system is flawed, it isn't just...it is rigged.
But not in the way that you might think.

Our hands are tied,
we cannot teach, we cannot guide.

Tell us how to run our households,
setting you up for a hard-ass life.
Can't take your phone, can't tell you no,
Can't raise you right, can't help you grow...
Can't give you a phone to save your life—

To be your lifeline
and be here for you if you need an escape.
If you are unsure or need an ear
so instead, you sit at your visit, alone and in fear.

Too afraid of legalities,
We are forced to give in to the powers that be.

We give up on the kids that need us now
by submitting to circumstance...
We let time go by...we push issues aside
Without looking back, with no second glance.

Then time runs out, and we wonder why
They choose to age out instead of try,
When all this time,
we could have been working on a wonderful life!

Too afraid of manipulation to take any type of action…
Controlled by chaos. The chaos wins.
If we constantly worry what birth mom thinks,
What the worker thinks—what the foster mom thinks.
Instead of what the child needs.

This is where the focus should always be.
All the while we speak of normalcy.
But what is best for the child?
Sometimes it isn't black and white.
We gotta fight!
And realize we are all on the same team.

Society deserves for us to give this our all
Because when we fail and the child ages out,
Society steps in and figures it out
For them…
Since we failed to do
what the system should be designed to do.

I really think we need to take each foster case as an individual case to analyze. There is no cookie-cutter solution. Sometimes, a child is left home alone so a single parent can go try to find a job. This goes back to the poverty cycle where a person can't advance because the system of law is against them. Survival mode steps in, and maybe someone does something stupid like sell drugs to survive. Then this puts them in jail, the child is taken away, and they have to sell their house and move to a less secure area. This never-ending cycle is just so damn hard to get out of.

There are people out there willing to step up and help these families out of the situation they are in. My husband and I try to not just help the child who comes into our home but also the entire family. This is one of our contributions to the world...one way in which we use ourselves to help the world. And in every bad event, rotten circumstance, or dreadful tragedy, there are people raising their hands and their voices to correct the wrong.

Some other pretty amazing people have entered my life, and some left just as quickly. My biggest regret is not getting contact info for some pretty prominent people who have helped mold me over the years. From the supportive drunk girl I met in the bathroom when I was upset over a guy leaving with another girl (who told me I was beautiful and to never settle), to bosses, teachers, and friends who have come and gone—so many people have played a part in who I am today. Some will always remain strangers, but I have accepted that as the way it was meant to be.

My biggest findings in recent years have been to only surround myself with people who are on my team. I'm so careful about who I let into my circle, and I am very quick to take people out of my life who are not really there for me. Yes, there are some nasty people who roam this world, but if we look for the good, we can only see what Jesus intended—for us to be His hands and feet. His hands and feet are all around. We just have to open our eyes and we can see the good, even in the hardest of times.

I believe that tragedy and hard times connect us all. We are all connected by the services we are willing to do to help others in need. When the world is dark, and we are having a hard time making it through the day, maybe we are having a hard time seeing the light. And it may be during these times that we need to BE the light.

The Plan

Suicide. Hate in the streets,
Massacres, car wrecks, death, murder,
Overdoses, babies dying in car seats.
Explosions, shootings, cancer, robbery,
Rape, pandemic, illness, floods, war.
Buildings collapsing, corrupt government,
Hurricanes and tornadoes, pedophiles next door.

In all of this,
There are people all around
Making a safe place for you and your kids.
Search and rescue teams,
Food pantries, shelters,
Volunteers, and good Samaritans.
Those running toward danger
In order to make a difference.
Standing up for equality,
Defending the right to live, to love, and to exist.
Providing medical attention,
Making deep connections.

Just six degrees of separation between all of us,
A network of relationships.
Paths are crossed, roads intersect,
And at just the right time,
Shackles release and the opportunity arises
For aid and comfort,
And love and light.

We will all get through this,
There's no other choice.

And when we don't see the good,
We must radiate.
Use our hands and feet, lift our voice.
We will come out of this darkness together,
Hand in hand.
By doing. By being.
It's all a part of the plan.

I have learned to see the world through the people around me. I surround myself with good people. I see the good all around me, and sometimes, that is all I focus on. If I tried to focus on the ugly going on in the entire world, I wouldn't sleep at night.

So instead, I look for what I can find in my own state, my own town, my own city, and my own block. I start small. If we all do our part in the space around us, then we would create a wonderful world.

We encounter amazing people everywhere we go. Just look for them. Find them amidst the chaos. They are there.

Self-Reflection:

1. Reflect on people who have come and gone in your life. Who stands out as being good to and for you?

____

____

____

____

____

2. If they are still alive, write the good people you have identified
a letter or pick up the phone and tell them just how much they
meant to you in that particular moment of your life.

____

____

____

____

____

chapter **11**

THOU SHALT ACCEPT YOUR JOURNEY TO FIND SELF-CONTENTMENT

I belong to a group of women veterans called WoVeN. Recently, we had a meeting, and our discussion fell on self-esteem. We talked about how we view ourselves, which pieces we allow the public to see and which ones we hide from those around us. In addition, we discussed our areas of growth and our greatest accomplishments. We then said out loud our favorite part about ourselves.

From there, the conversation turned, and we then discussed how we would describe the other group members. We talked about what we learned from them and our favorite things about them. The twenty-year-old me would not have been able to handle the feedback. So much positivity thrown at me would have sent me down a path of thinking I didn't deserve those kind words to be spoken to or about me. But here I was, finding myself agreeing with them and thanking them.

———

For a long time, I was running in circles, repeating my hot mess over and over again. I ended up down a dark road throughout my early journey more than a handful of times. The same damn dark alley with no street lights, no flowers, no good people looking out for me, and no grandmas meeting me at their door to give me cookies. It felt dark and desolate.

During that time in my life when I turned to boys and sex whenever I felt bad about myself, I thought it would make me feel better. That is where I sought love and contentment. But it never did satisfy me. Then I turned to alcohol to dull my feelings. I also cut myself. All of these self-medicating habits led me to this same dark alley over and over.

It wasn't until I had my first-born child, my innocent son, that I had some kind of epiphany. I realized that while I did these self-destructive things that led me to produce fatherless children (which we all know defined me a lot of my life), I didn't have to also force them to walk down THEIR journeys without a father figure. They didn't have to have an absent mother, either. So that very day, October 2nd, 2004, is when I began this journey of acknowledging that I'd been going down these same dark roads and I had to do something to change my future paths. I realized that I wasn't happy with myself and kept trying to find contentment in places I had no business looking. I had to grant myself permission and favor to move through this.

So, I started a new path of acceptance. My fun, sunny highway of life didn't begin until I accepted both the things I could control AND the things I had no control over. I had to give myself consent to receive and examine the shit that happened. I couldn't let it define my self-worth. I couldn't begin my healing process—and I couldn't proceed with a plan of loving myself—until I accepted that YES, I made some dumb moves in life. With this acceptance, I also had to analyze the choices that I had made and the decisions I needed to make that would lead me down a better trail.

That was step one of many steps that made up this journey to find self-contentment. Even though being a mom wasn't a part of my plan at that moment, it definitely stopped me in my tracks and made me consider the journey I was on and how it would impact my child and our futures.

While on this path of finding acceptance in my journey and ultimately of myself, I had to empower my imperfect self. I came to grips with my past. I wined and dined my flaws and blemishes. I cradled my faults and weaknesses. I permitted myself to be human and make mistakes. I let go of the perfect vision of who I thought I should be, and I tolerated the notion that I needed to consent to award myself grace when needed.

I sometimes act like I am steel and that I have no feelings. I act like nothing can penetrate me or break me down. So while I may seem like I have my shit together, there are always times I revert back to this scared, lonely little girl, and it is a battle I have to fight within myself often. I have learned that when I am afraid, it is usually because I just don't have enough information, or I am not confident enough and need to learn more. Because of this, I am a learnaholic! I crave more knowledge.

Sometimes, I sign up for so many classes that I overbook my schedule and end up not being able to handle it all. Then, I get overwhelmed because I try to do too much. I am still working on this, too. I mentioned this early as a possible addiction. I get a high from the feeling of being overwhelmed. I am aware that I do this. So far, I haven't sabotaged myself with this. I move a lot and change jobs a lot. I add things to my schedule. Each time, at least so far, I've found better opportunities and do better for myself. But I am aware and still monitoring. I accept this part of me, and I work on myself often.

I still often have a hard time trusting people. I have a deep feeling that I don't need anyone. I have a hard time asking anyone for help and will damn near kill myself to get everything done for myself, by myself. With an absentee father, and my mother working all the time, I had no friends. Sex was just taken from me at times. Because of what followed after I left my ex-husband, I have learned the skill of extreme independence. I was wounded, betrayed, and very hurt throughout moments in my life. Being overly independent is a defense strategy from being let down so much in life. I am a giver and felt like everyone in my life would take but never give back in return. Escaping extreme independence is something I continue to work on.

Another thing I have learned about myself is that I overshare. I will tell anything to anyone. In my mind, if I tell everything and wear my life on my sleeve, no one can go behind my back or try to ruin me from the outside in. My husband and my children constantly tell me to zip it because I share too much. I accept this about myself, and I am still working on this.

When I finally analyzed where I was in regards to loving ME, that was a game-changer to a brighter, "funner" road to travel with MYSELF. But I had to acknowledge that, by becoming hardened, I was actually hurting myself in the end. I put this guard up so I wouldn't become hurt when other people judged me. Or I could say to myself that I didn't care if they valued me based on what I was doing because I had this power inside of me, and no one could take that from me.

I have inspired myself to be my own biggest damn cheerleader. I am my biggest advocate and my biggest supporter. If anyone was going to choose the right path for me, it's going to be me! And by making good decisions for myself, I am also in a position to alter how others perceive me.

Some say it is all about the journey and not the destination, but I think we have many destinations throughout our lifetime, and each one is important and worth striving for. Yes, the journey is important too, but so are the pauses we take when we just stand still. It is all important. And with each adversity, each stumbling block, and at each intersection we come to, we have to make heavy decisions for ourselves. Do we go left or go right? Do we keep returning to that dark crossroads repeatedly, or do we take a leap of faith and go down the unknown road that could lead to a content life?

I know I cannot erase the awful choices I made in life. I don't want my son to see me as the person I used to be when the fact of the matter was, from the very moment I found out I was going to be a mom, I wasn't her anymore. I wasn't a lost soul with a deep void. My abyss was filled the day I saw that positive sign on that stick. I decided that day that not only did he fill that hole for me, but I also made it a life goal to never be a reason he had this parent-sized mass missing from his being.

Our travels are made up of little moments, and each moment could be considered a destination. When we complete an item from our list of things that make us happy, we are reaching a destination. When we complete an item from our list of ways to pay it forward/random acts of kindness, we are making stops along our path to reach each fate determined for us and by us.

Each person that roams this earth has their own journey. They have their own intersections and decisions to make. They fall into their own pits at times, and they get on their own planes when needed. Do not compare your trips around the sun to anyone else's. I only say this because I spent so much of my time comparing myself to where those around me were in their lives. I thought, *This friend was raised by both parents. That friend was engulfed with so much love.* I sometimes grew envious of others and what they had. But the fact remains that they, at some time in their lives, went through hard times. And we all have power over how we overcome the trials we face.

And dammit, I am an overcomer!

My journey is made of a lot of small steps. Some steps forward, some backward. Some steps are into a field of flowers and some in a pile of dog shit.

I try to break things down into small things. I think about my daily habits, my routines, and what control I have over myself. What type of woman I want to be and what baby steps I need to take to get there. I didn't become who I am overnight. I am me through the steps I take and the days I live. I have built myself into who I am. After all, Rome wasn't built in a day. But you know what? Every day, people were working on that empire...bricks were being laid day after day. Skills were being learned, and it took time to create sovereignty.

I had to master being intentional and falling in love with the path I am on. I resort to my list of things that make me happy and my list of ways to pay it forward often. I call these lists my RESETS because when I am feeling bad and maybe even venturing down a long, unknown road, I can always regroup and ground myself back to something known that makes me content. These two lists are my basis of being in charge of my own self-contentment.

You will find those two lists to be powerful resources in accepting the road you travel. The more you sprinkle items from those lists into your life, the better your travels can be. Ultimately, you are in charge of whether you live life to the fullest or not. When you are living your fullest purpose, you won't have time to look left or right; you will go whatever direction the wind takes you, and those are ALWAYS the best destinations!

I won't even waste a second beating myself up over a decision I made or didn't make in my past. Life is too short and too fragile to ever think, *If only I would have done that differently.* If I ever think that I didn't do the right thing, I just reevaluate, reroute, and head in a different direction. It is rare to make a mistake so great that we can't take corrective action and create a new path.

I traveled a long way in time to get to this level of "I don't give a fuck" that I currently find myself on. And I have never been more at peace. I haven't always accepted my journey, but it was entirely freeing when I finally made the decision to just acknowledge that my migration was mine alone. My voyage is my responsibility, and no matter why I make decisions to choose one path over another, no one else has that control over me. I did this on my own, and I can run in circles if I want to, but those are my choices. I now welcome the next crossroad and the liberating decisions that come with it. But, oh, what a road I have traveled to get to this very moment.

The Road I Traveled to Find Contentment
This road of life that I have traveled
To get to where I am right now,
It wasn't an easy road to navigate,
But I've made it to this point somehow.

At times, this route was rugged and rough,
with potholes, craters, and deep depressions.
This path has flooded more than once.
I've needed to take detours,
I've run into roadblocks. I've hit heavy obstructions.

I've even had to backtrack and make new paths along the way.
The road had many twists and bends,
Countless uphills, a myriad of downhills,

But through it all, I've made it to my journey's end.

I've traveled this road alone mostly,
For no one can travel it but me.
I had no idea where I would end up!
But here I am, filled with self-certainty.

My final destination is calm, peaceful, smooth,
With flowers on the sides,
Gardens and trees all around,
And the sun always shines.

This I will maintain. This is where I'll stay.
I have found self-contentment.
I feel replete with serenity.

I have decided to let hard choices, bad decisions and, road-blocks bring me strength. All throughout my life, I have made decisions based on my life experiences, and each time, I come out stronger than before. I've learned to push past defeat to find success in all facets of life—mental, emotional, physical and spiritual.

Whatever your definition of success is, only you can find it. Being successful has a different meaning to each and every one of us. Some will run big corporations. Some will start nonprofits. Some will be housewives. When a person feels led to do certain things, they don't place their will on what society drills in us as success. A nomad traveling doing mission work finds success in how many people he can help. A teacher finds purpose in how many children can find knowledge. A pastor finds success in how many souls he can help find Jesus. We all have our own path to follow, and we all have our own calling. Don't be ashamed of your life choices and decisions. You had to go through it to get to where you are. Each decision you make will lead you to fulfilling your purpose over and over again.

Sometimes, we are judged for our moments in time instead of the entire roadmap of our life. For instance, how many of you have driven down the street to see someone begging for help and have cast judgment on them? Or how many call someone less valuable because they decided to move in with their parents as an adult and take some time off work because they needed time for themselves? For some, whether forcefully or purposefully, we need just a moment of time to pause. Rest. Be still. Even if just to regroup and renew. And we may not like it at the time, especially if it's a forced pause, but I'd bet if it was forced upon you, it was needed for one reason or another. Besides, Exodus 14:14 says, "The Lord will fight for you, you need only to be still." So be still is what I do when I don't know what else to do. I pause.

It goes without saying that sometimes we go through something for the sole purpose of helping someone else through it. That's okay! Use your journey to help others. Your story could save someone's life! We may not realize in the midst of going through turmoil, but in the future, it just hits us sometimes when we are in conversation with a stranger, going through something we have dealt with, or when our child faces something. This "AHA" moment catches us when we realize, *Hey—I've had the same experience and here is what I learned from it!*

We all go through shit. Some are more open about their history than others. Some flaunt it around on the sleeves of their shirts. But whatever you do, just don't be a prisoner inside your own mind. Romans 12:2 says, "Do not conform to the pattern of this world, but be transformed by the renewing of your mind." Your mind is a powerful thing. All behavior and internal changes begin in the mind.

Your story is your story. Find freedom in using your story to benefit others. Talk about it. Be open to sharing your successes and your failures. And know that God will use your story for His glory, even if it doesn't seem so polished or glorious while you are experiencing your pitfalls.

I had to make a decision to not worry about how others perceive me during flashes in time and accept the journey I have been on to get to my huge accomplishments or my big moments that define me. In doing this, I released myself from the bondage I placed on myself.

Not My Own Prisoner

If I place all of my worry into how others perceive me,
I become a prisoner...captive inside of me.

To be set free, I must grasp that the drive in me is bound
Primarily by love.

Family is not simply blood...
Friends are not solely association...
A SHARED love must subsist.

Therefore, to impress pardon on myself,
I must aspire to surround myself
Exclusively by those who find enjoyment in
Companionship with me.

To remain content, I must let go of those
Who fail to lift me up and rather attempt to break me down.

For if I have no love for myself,
how can I expect others to recognize

The grace and awe, the fulfilling esteem...
The raw beauty found inside of me?

I realize that I cannot uncover happiness...
I must contrive it...I must create it...I must devise it...

I avow that my chains are not implemented by others
But are imposed upon myself.

I shall decide to fixate my energy on those deserving.
I shall decide to let go of those causing detriment.
I shall decide that my innermost happiness
is found within myself.
And I shall determine with whom I will meld and integrate with.

If you cannot bear amity, relations shall be averted.
I seek peace...I seek wholeness...I seek contentment...
And it shall all be found within...

I take off my shackles...
I liberate myself from bondage...I satisfy my soul...
I hold high regard for myself...I embrace who I am...

I am ME...in myself, I am FREE.

I've been redeemed by accepting my journey. It took me a long time to get here, but here I am. I am content, and I want nothing more than to be a source to help others feel this same SAVAGE contentment.

I wish I had immaculate, all-powerful knowledge to drop on you, but literally my life changed just by accepting the journey I had already walked, not holding grudges over myself for the stupid decisions I made in life, and moving forward with purpose and love. It was that simple for me.

It does help to have puppies and kittens on your journey. But that is just a bonus.

Self-Reflection:

1. Your assignment for this chapter is simple. Just reflect on and accept where you are and how you got here. Life isn't all daisies, but realize hardships sometimes have to happen to get to where you are. If you aren't where you want to be yet, understand that you have to be in this very moment to prepare you to get to where you are going next. Journal your thoughts in this space:

____

____

____

____

____

2. Part of accepting my journey of where I have been is also considering where I want to be and how I will continue to be my source of self-contentment. Write your bucket list in the spaces below. Think long and hard about achievements, experiences, travels, etc., that you wish to accomplish in your lifetime, something that really makes you happy that you have always wanted

to do but haven't had the chance yet. Write it down in the space provided.

____

____

____

____

____

3. Now write out a plan for your journey on how you will check this item off of your bucket list. Think of what you will travel in, what you will eat, and where you will stay. What could go wrong? How can you overcome what might go wrong? How will you accept anything that might go wrong in this part of your journey? The key to acceptance is to not go down dark roads over and over again but to create a new path that is fun and brings contentment.

____

____

____

____

____

birth canal—passageway
to life

THOU SHALT TAKE TIME TO ENJOY
THE PAUSE

There is a song by Jonny Diaz called "Breathe" that has become somewhat of a life motto to me. The tempo is all over the place; it goes very fast and during those moments my heart is racing and my mind is going crazy. This part of the song parallels my life. Busy, chaotic, fast-paced, and intense.

Then, it gets to the chorus and it slows way down. While repeating *breathe, just breathe*, there is a slow heartbeat in the background. During these parts of the song, my heart is calm and my mind is quiet and lucid. I am at peace. This chorus is very specific, and it is a calling from a higher being to just rest. The chorus encourages me to set all of the craziness of everyday life aside and become a better being by being still. Hear the stillness for yourself at:

https://www.youtube.com/watch?v=hnjeMwxFuBA

We are human. Our souls and our spirits get tired and weary, and we must take the needed time to root ourselves in self-care. We have to stand up for ourselves and lay down all the busyness to tame ourselves and find balance. Every minute of every day cannot be crazy busy. If it was, we would give out, and what good are we to anyone else if we let that happen?

I am sharing this advice for myself, too. Yes, I run a hundred miles an hour at all times. It has been a struggle to provide self-care and take pauses. I had to really reboot and focus on why I need to take time for myself in order to be my best me for when someone I love or someone I don't know needs me. I work hard to make sure I am squared away and happy. I work hard to maintain my savage happiness. I am in tune with myself—so much so that the second things don't feel right, I am real quick to start my journey of stepping in a different direction, taking a pause, or starting over. And I utilize tools and resources I found for myself, like my list of things that make me happy and my list of ways to pay it forward. These are vital to me and parts of my daily life. Taking pauses has become a part of my everyday life, too.

While I don't hear a voice speak down to me, telling me to be still or rest or breathe, life has many designed elements that cue me to do so. When it is light out and the sun is shining, I am busy, moving, exploring, and living. And when the sun goes down and it gets dark outside, that is my signal to start finishing what I started so I can wind down for the evening. The darkness kickstarts my body to produce melatonin, and the nightly cycle begins for me to seek rest.

There's also a calmness about being in nature. The sound of the birds chirping or the waves crashing. Witnessing the slowness of a turtle or feeling the warmth of a puppy kiss. Lying in the darkness and counting the stars or making shapes from the clouds. There is perfection in the design of the world if only we take a moment to look around and see it.

I believe in the alignment of the universe. Signs, shall we say. Luke 21:25 says, "There will be signs in the sun, moon, and stars. On the earth, nations will be in anguish and perplexity at the roaring and tossing of the sea." And Psalm 104:19 says, "He made the moon to mark the seasons, and the sun knows when to go down." Nature has a way of showing us things we may not hear in words. It's magical.

When I worked for the real estate tech company and was told I was too comma happy, at first, I was upset at the critique. My boss told me not every pause warrants a comma and that I didn't need to use so many commas in my writing.

After thinking about this, I now love the phrase *comma happy* and use it in life often. While she meant it in a somewhat negative way, it makes me feel good inside. A comma is a pause in a sentence. And yes, I have been known to use a lot of them because I enjoy taking dramatic pauses. A lot. I love the phrase so much that I once built a limo company and named it Comma Happy Limo Services. Our catchphrase was, *"Take a pause from your everyday grind and promenade on a grandeur joy ride."* I literally created a business idea around taking a pause from life to get out there and enjoy the ride!

Sometimes, even in the midst of the chaos going on around me, during a very bad day, or a particularly hard time in my life, I have learned to stop—to pause and reflect. I have learned not to react and to give it some time. Most of the time, it doesn't take long for me to figure out why something happened. Everything happens for a reason, and when I keep that in mind, I can't allow myself to stress over something because I know that it was meant to happen.

For instance, when I found out I was pregnant during such an unstable time for me, I didn't understand it. After all, we were careful. How could this have happened? But I genuinely believe my son saved me from myself.

And when I went through an awful divorce, it was such a dark time for me, but it moved me to Virginia, to a place aligned just for me to be able to meet my husband. I know I wouldn't be where I am today if I hadn't chosen him as my life partner. His entire being is like no other person I have ever met on this earth, and life is so much better just having him in it.

It has taken me a long time to learn this life hack of being still in the midst of turmoil. Sometimes, this required me to shut out the world while I worked on myself. Sometimes, I requested the aid of those close to me to help me have a moment to rest. But taking pauses has become a part of my everyday life.

Pausing also means knowing when to bite my tongue. I've always been one to spit out whatever comes to mind as soon as it pops into my head without even thinking twice. Part of enjoying the pause is also stopping in my tracks when something upsets me, being mindful, thinking about it, putting myself in the other person's shoes, and giving it some time before I respond or react. That definitely doesn't come naturally to me, and I had to work very hard at this. It not only shows growth and control, but it also has made life easier because I am not having to clean up unintentional messes from my big mouth.

In foster care, there is a term called "respite care." This just means that a break is needed for both the child and the foster parents, and there are licensed homes that the child can go to for a weekend or however long is needed. This rest is much-needed at times. And my husband and I have both needed respite care and have been the home providing respite care. There is no shame in needing a pause and a reset within the home. We all need that time for ourselves.

I mentioned at the beginning that I am a musical person. I played the violin and sang in the choir all throughout middle school and high school. It was a huge part of my life growing up. And I will say that the pauses between the notes are just as important as the notes themselves. It creates drama and necessary attention from the listener. Sometimes, our pauses in life are designed to demand attention for ourselves. And often, a pause is a necessity.

<u>LIVE in the Pauses</u>

SLOW DOWN.
Take a pause,
Gather your thoughts,
Don't discuss
Your private matters
Or your inner afflictions
Until you have thought it through.

TAKE TIME.
Meditate,
Collect yourself,
Know who you are
Before you embark
On an important journey,
Warrior that you are.

REST and BE STILL.
It's vital to your health.
Time will wait.
The moments tomorrow
Will reinstate,
And the chaos of today will
Dissipate
If you only pause
In the name of self-love.

TAKE THE TIME

To live in the pauses
Sprinkled all throughout your life.
You will find
That is where the true adventure lies.

Life is so good when you take the time to actively live and enjoy life while throwing in some pauses at just the right time. Rest! You deserve it, and your soul needs it.

Self-Reflection:

1. What are some ways that you relax, rest, and take pauses in life? For instance, some things I like to do are: enjoy my morning coffee, listen to music, cuddle with my kitties and puppies, take a walk, and breathe in nature. List some things you do in the spaces provided:

____

____

____

____

____

____

2. What are some active steps you can take to unplug and unwind when needed? When I am having trouble sleeping or even concentrating, I have to disconnect from social media and electronics in general. I have learned to time block and only look

at my emails and such during specific times. What are some things you can do to shut off the world in times when you need a break?

____

____

____

____

____

____

3. Try to time block, and choose one of the activities that you just wrote down in number two at least once a day. It will help you value your time and help other people in your life value your time, too. Self-care is so important.

my rebirth

chapter 13

THOU SHALT START OVER (AGAIN
AND AGAIN IF NECESSARY)

Recently, I got a call at 7:30 in the morning from a client. She wasn't just any client, though. She was a previous employee's mom who was helping me find a home for my employee (who worked at my CBD store)—a home that she could call hers. A home that might have helped her find stability and a place of comfort to get her through her hard cycles. You see, Zoey—and I don't mention actual names very often in this book, but her name had meaning—Zoey means LIFE. Zoey was so full of life. She was vibrant and had energy inside of her and surrounding her that I have never seen before.

Her mom called me to tell me that Zoey passed away during the night, and she had to make some hard decisions to remove her from life support and donate her organs as she had wanted.

I don't cry often, but this had me in shambles.

Zoey had always been an open book, and she used her life experiences to help others. She was the first to tell people she had a mental illness and was really trying to overcome it. She would coach my foster children. She would talk about her struggles, and she would get to a point where she was making progress. And when she felt herself slipping, she would take steps in different directions. She would start over when she needed to, recently going to other states to try to better herself. Or maybe to try to get away from herself. Whatever her reasons were, she was doing it to save herself.

I'm not sure what ultimately took her life. What is so hard for me to grasp is that the very day she left this world, she was reaching out to me for help. I didn't realize it at the time because she did it in her Zoey way—full of life. She was asking for some hours at the store. I told her she wouldn't want what I had to give because they weren't regular hours as I just needed help as a fill-in. She graciously wanted anything she could get.

Last year, her work performance was slipping. I helped as much as I could, but it was affecting business. I didn't fire her; I simply told her to get herself straight, then come back, and I would welcome her with open arms. Since then, she had other job opportunities. She started over again and again, each time trying to create a different scenario.

Ultimately, her life was cut short because she was overtaken by something she couldn't escape. A beautiful soul with so much heart and so much talent, she was needed in this world, but the world wasn't ready. I mourn the loss of her and will honor the life she lived.

And shortly after I got this phone call from her mother, I got another call from a lender to whom I sent some of my real estate clients.

He told me that a client I sent to him chose to find another real estate agent because of some things they saw on my Facebook page. The client stated that I am pro-Black. To him, I seemed to be anti-white because I had a post from an AP U.S. History teacher who didn't understand why people defend the Confederate flag. This teacher went into detail about when this flag started flying over government buildings, what this symbol meant, what was being taught in our schools, and how history was seemingly being rewritten because it is uncomfortable.

I looked at the potential client's page. He believes writing "Black Lives Matter" on the streets of D.C. is threatening our democracy and causing racial divide. He made posts saying that kids live in poverty here in America but Democrats were fighting for "illegals" instead of worrying about the people already here. As if one life is any more important than another. A life in need is a life in need. Regardless of where they are from. He had many posts of Black-on-Black crime, saying, "Where is the outrage?" And he was upset about the Confederate statues coming down.

I am pro-Black. That does not mean I am anti-white. I am white. My husband is white. I birthed two white boys of my own from my body and I birthed a Black daughter from my body. I also delivered white, Indian, Latino and Black babies through surrogacy. As a mother, I will always fight for my daughter to have a good life. I want her to have a life where she is free to explore, make mistakes and learn from them, and find success. I believe all of these are things that are hard for a Black person in America today. The very fact that I lost a client over this proves that.

Yes, I am hurt that I lost real estate business for the reasons provided. But I sleep well at night knowing that I am on the side of what's right in this country, and if I have to struggle to demonstrate my need to love and protect my daughter and people who look like her, I will take the punches thrown at me. I will start over again and again and stand up over and over to pave the way to achieve equality in this country.

That is my dream.

<u>Dirty Money</u>
I was fired today by a client because
My pro-Black stance apparently means anti-white.
My white husband and my white children
birthed by my white body
My white body that also birthed my Black baby, too.
I was fired today because they don't like when I say
The Confederate flag stands for white supremacy.
It symbolizes hate.
So many lives torn apart under this flying rag.
I read comments today that said this flag represents peace
Because under this flag, one side fought to end slavery,
They didn't realize that one side also fought to keep it.
The side that lost still flies this in hostility.
They saw on my Facebook that I stand with my fist in the air.
For my child that I bore.
Chanting "BLACK LIVES MATTER"
For the whole world to hear.
You know what I saw on their page?
They say the Democrats cause such a divide
By painting "BLACK LIVES MATTER" in the streets of D.C.
How could they leave that there
For all the world to see?
How dare they not clean their streets?
People are offended
That as they walk, they see THIS under their feet.
I got fired today and tears are streaming.
I don't want their dirty money.
I don't want their business if it means
Tolerating their gross hate for humanity.
I got fired today, and while it's okay for me...
I'll dry my face, rise up, and face

The hate spewed at the Black and Brown races.
This act towards me is nothing compared
To what they face on a daily basis.
I bow down and kneel in peace.
I'm on the side of humankind.
I've signed my name for equal opportunity.
I'm taking a much-needed break.
A COMMA HAPPY of sorts.
To clear my head, process the discriminate.
Then, back at it, doing what I do.
This isn't anything new for me.
I've always been in the side of what's right.
If I had to do it again, I would do it all the same.
I'll defend my daughter's honor every single day.
The right to live in this world
In equality.
For the clients I have lost, another will come.
But it doesn't make this easy.
A battle I face
As I raise my daughter in a world of hate.
Throwing their dirty money
Only where their narrative is met.
I was fired today. Still, I stand tall.
Fist closed. Held high.
Prejudice exposed.
Dirty money thrown into the wind
Until all can be blinded by the color of skin.

Yes, I cried my eyes out over this. But this event fueled me to fight harder than ever before for a society where Black and Brown boys, and Black and Brown girls have a fighting chance. Where we don't run right to other wrongs and try diversion tactics when talking about how Black people are treated in America. Where a person isn't seen as "the illegal" but as a person hoping for a new start. And right now, my purpose is to fight this good fight for my daughter, a child growing up in an unfair world.

I read something the other day that stopped me in my tracks. It basically said that each person who meets me has a different version of me in their minds, and it's very different from what I think about myself. It further said that the person I think I am doesn't even exist outside of my mind.

WOW! Deep, right?

This is because I am the only person on this earth that has a full and complete understanding of me. Everyone else just gets bits and pieces. Some only see my struggles, while some see me for my great successes. Some only knew me during a rebuild and some knew me when I was flourishing. That very thought took my breath away.

But I can't stop on that one thought alone. I can't let it consume me. I am always in a state of transition. Like a river, I am ever-flowing, never stagnant. I am rising, flourishing, sometimes falling. Occasionally, I am at rock bottom, and then I am rebuilding again.

I strive for bigger and better things at all times. Even when I am seemingly on top of the world, I know there is still way higher I can go. And especially when I am on low ground, I know there is nowhere to go but up. I am never the same version of myself to anyone. I accept that. I wish everyone saw me the way I saw me, but it's okay that they don't. They see me the way they are supposed to see me. The way they need to see me. I weave in and out of people's lives at just the right time, and I go just the same. My journey is my own, and each transition was destined.

<u>Transitioning</u>

So many times I've had to start over,
Sometimes without closure,
Sometimes no reasons,
Sometimes no faults, at times, my own,
With no one but me to blame.
Occasionally, it was just my season,
My time to withstand the rain...

New beginnings aren't always a bad thing.
We get knocked down to begin again,
Rebuild, restructure, restore, and redefine
Only to turn out better the second time.
Sometimes, I have to lose myself to find me again,
Only to improve, triumph, overcome, and overtake.
I cultivate within myself,
Seeds are planted, and I await...
I am my own uprising.

At times, I'm forced to my knees
With no choice but to get grounded,
Rooted...ready to begin my ascension,
To reclaim my victory,
Leave the old me in history,
Give birth to a better version of me,
Upgraded, updated, and reconstructed
Transcended...the sky is my limit.
But why stop there?

Flourishing, blooming, blossoming,
Emerging into the ether.
Further and further, reestablishing me...

Each time, I am different, and each time, I rise.
Even if the old me dies,
I prepare my field, fertilize...
Fostering a heightened me.

I'm an old oak tree with all my layers,
Each ring marking my progression.
I'm my creator, I reclaim my rising,
Going higher each time.
My transformation flawless,
Yet at the same time, I'm a work in progress.
Always transitioning
Into each new and intended version of me.

Everything I have been through has led me to this very moment, which leads me to the next. Even right now, in this very place in time, I am only on a stepping stone to my next destination. When I fall, I get back up and take my life back, over and over again. It happens to the best of us.

There was a time in my life when I had good intentions. I was having baby after baby for other people in need, but I was neglecting myself. I was letting myself go and did so in the name of helping others. It was consuming me. I was gaining weight, and I kept telling myself it was okay because it was for a worthy cause.

And then, one day, I got sucker-punched with a hiatal hernia. I had it operated on and then could only drink my food for almost nine months. I lost roughly 100 pounds forcefully. So yes, it was a forced restart, but one that was so needed.

Take My Life Back

I'm a prisoner in my skin, captive to my thoughts.
Can't let nobody in, I think about what I'm not.
My body doesn't work, I'm a vegetable in this place.
My mind absorbs it in, not to be erased
I want to be active, but my body has been beat down.
I put it through hell, I didn't care...in the name of life,
adding pound after pound
But I MUST FIND WILL...INSIDE...MYSELF

The bigger I get, the more I wallow in food
My mind is fucked up, I retreat in solitude...
Financial need put me in this place.
Baby after baby, I kept telling myself, *I'm doing a good thing,*
But when I look in the mirror, I don't recognize my own face
My body is paying the price, and inside I'm burning...
I AM...ON...FIRE.

My mind is taking the toll, but I'll continue to smile through my
sacrifice.
Can I get back to health? Feel more alive?
All the wealth in the world doesn't fix the damage done.
It's gonna take hard work, I'll have to step out of myself,
Get out of my own way, and out of my head,
Make the decision to not fall into death...
I must SAVE...MY...OWN...LIFE.

I have so much to live for, this life I have made,
I want to watch my kids live, and grow, and slay!
They breathe life into me, it is me who needs them!
They fill me with calm, I will overcome!
I won't let myself fall back into a hole,

But today's a new day to be daring and bold.
I will change my circumstance,
create a fortress others want to see,
But more importantly...
A home I am happy to be in, a sanctuary
And NOW...IS...THE...TIME.

I reclaim my life back, break out of the chains,
Take back my rein...
I have a lot of life left, it's gonna be the best yet!
I'll dance in the rain, travel, and explore...
Do all the things I couldn't do before.
I'll never look back, that chapter has ended unless it's to learn.
Right here and right now, I stop making excuses...
This new fire inside is a wonderful burn...
Slowly, I do this
ONE...STEP...AT...A...TIME.
I've done it before—I'll do it again...

I have learned we have seasons in life. We are constantly in a state of transition. Life is ever-moving and we are ever-changing. One day, we wake up and we cross over the threshold of waiting to a moment of completion, and then, we are back to planning and preparing. Our cycles of life are designed in such a way that each individual step we take sometimes doesn't make sense until we get through it, look back, and then think, *AHA! That's why I went through that!*

I realize throughout my life I have found myself over and over again. I have lost myself sometimes but it is important to note that when I lost myself, I always seemed to find myself again.

I've been blessed each step of my journey. Even when I was in the pit of it and I didn't feel blessed—I WAS BLESSED! I've always been cared for in one way or another. Even when I wasn't looking out for myself, someone always stepped in to handle things for me until I woke the hell up and got my shit together.

I'll be honest and say I am a Sagittarius. I am wild and free. A lot of times, I make rash, spontaneous decisions. I am independent and don't rely on others. Most of my restarts are BOOM—IN YOUR FACE!

But some of my most subtle choices have been the most life-transforming.

Just saying yes to invitations has sometimes been life-changing. I've met some pretty fantastic people by leaving my house when I didn't want to, like my good friend I met at church or my sweet friend I met at a networking event. Not many get the title of "friend" in my life. It takes a special person. But I have met some pretty incredible people just by taking small chances and getting out of the house. And some people I met have led to amazing life opportunities.

Little things help me in my starting over process, like finding my favorite scent of perfume, incense, or candle. Or listening to the radio and landing on a life-changing song. Finding a good space to think when I need time to myself. A favorite comfy pair of pants. My blanket. Maybe they get me to a place where my mind is right and I can start thinking of actions to take. These small things kick-started me and really helped me through life. And being at a good place mentally is so important when making decisions for yourself. I'm in my comfort zone when I have one of these things that I have found I like. The kind of comfort that pushes me to the next step.

Sometimes, the hardest part in life is knowing when to be still and when to take action. But either you make decisions for yourself, or they are forced upon you. When you aren't still and you need to be, it will be forced on you in the form of getting sick to take a day off work or needing a hiatal hernia operation.

Sometimes in my life, I have had to fake it until I made it. I've had to push on even when I didn't feel like I could. Sometimes, I have had to reach out for help. The people around us have been meticulously placed there for our specific times of need. I have no doubts about that. It is all a part of the plan for our lives. We just have to accept our journeys and go with the punches and the high-fives. We will always have good and bad thrown at us in waves. Sometimes, starting over is just changing our minds or doing something different.

But regardless, I'm in charge of my own damn story. I've hit a wall over and over throughout life. But if I would have given up, who knows where I would be now. I've lived it all, but I refuse to stay there or let it define me. I'm not ashamed of any of it.

An old Arab proverb says, "Sunshine all the time makes a desert." The rain is so necessary for life! Learn to dance in times of rain. That is the only way to survive.

This is Me

I'm impulsive and wild...carefree, no fucks to give.
Also me—I care too much and want to save the world, ALL OF IT
At the same time. Right now. I'm impatient.

I'm distinctive.
I'm the black sheep. Unusual. Offbeat. Radical. Unconventional.
Unique.
My heart cracks just a little every time I see
someone struggle or sad
or going through mess.
Sometimes, it stops me in my tracks,
and I'm worthless for the day.

And sometimes, I may seem so careless.
Calloused. Brutal. Insensitive. Heartless.
I can sometimes seem glacial.

I'm reckless. Sudden. Passionate.
If I see something I like, I get it
with no thought of what I will do with it.
I've wasted so much, and I never learn from it.
I squander too much.

Opposite of me—my husband will spend months
researching an item and never buy it,
Always in a state of ponder,
He will only make the decision to invest if he deems it perfect.
But perfection is deceptive. It never comes.

I don't care about perfection; I'm content with mediocrity.
I feel HARD and I'm LOUD at showing it.
If I am happy, you will know. If I am sad or mad, you will see.
I wear my heart on my sleeve.

This is me.
I care a lot. And I don't give a fuck.
All at the same time.

Sometimes, me saying "fuck" is me starting over. It's a part of life. Don't take it as defeat. Take it as just a part of your journey. You haven't lost anything by starting over, but sometimes, there is so much to gain by just scratching the entire thing and doing something entirely different.

. . .

Self-Reflection:

1. Think back on all of the times when you were at a very low place and couldn't see past your situation. As time went on and you got through it or started over, what new beginning came from it?

---

2. Maybe you feel stuck right now, at rock bottom, and you aren't sure what choices or decisions you need to make for yourself. What can you do to work on a new beginning and upward spiral to a renewed sense of life? What are some things going wrong for you right now, and what are some small steps you can take to move on? Where do you find comfort when making decisions for yourself?

---

3. Create a list of your favorite things. It will help remind you of where you can go to find peace when faced with the act of possibly needing to start over, big or small. Use this as a guide:

Scent____

Song____

Food____

Drink____

Ice Cream____

Color____

Animal____

Season____

Sport____

Activity/Hobby______________________________________

Book____

Flower____

Movie____

Place to go____

Place to shop____

Person____

When you are feeling stuck, at a crossroads, need to start over or make life changing decisions, get comfortable, look at this list, and pick some things from it to get yourself in a good headspace to make decisions for yourself. You are in charge of your destiny and have the power to alter your mind-frame. You can ultimately change the direction in which you are going, even during serious and hard times. Savage.

chapter 14a

THOU SHALT MAINTAIN HAPPINESS
WITHIN

As we approach this last chapter, I must tell you...the number fourteen holds special meaning to me. I was born December 14th, my husband was born August 14th, and we were married November 14th. So I knew I needed this book to have fourteen chapters. And here we are!! We made it!

> Author's Note: I realize there are two parts to this chapter, but I wanted to recognize the importance of maintaining happiness AND lifting up those around you to find happiness, while still maintaining the fourteen chapters.

I've talked about some pretty serious stuff throughout this book. I have faced challenges, and I have dealt with them and overcome them. As a result, I've learned a lot about myself over the years, and I am now at a place of maintaining my savage self-love and happiness. I've learned that I cannot find happiness in others; I can only find it within myself. Sometimes, I have to really dig deep in there to find it, but no one else has that control or power over me. Therefore, I would argue that maintaining happiness within myself is just as important as learning myself in the first place. Since my aura is all about giving in order to receive my bountiful blessings, **I just remember the acronym YOU BLESS.**

You fulfill your own needs.
Others matter too, so surround yourself with good people.
Use words wisely.

Be intentional.
Live in the NOW.
Exonerate yourself.
Serve.
Start over again and again if necessary.

Let's discuss.

YOU fulfill your own needs:

Fulfill your own needs. It's that simple. Be who and what you need. Don't rely on anyone else to handle your care. Own that responsibility! If you have been searching and searching for someone who can save you, fuck that! Save yourself. Never rely on someone else or put that much power in someone else's hands.

Happiness is an inside job. If you don't like where you are now, MOVE. YOU have the power over your life. You are not rooted where you are. You are not stuck. Pick yourself up and do something different. If freedom is what you seek, BE FREE! Get away. Obviously, you can't get away from yourself; just don't get in your own way. If your big dream is to be a good wife and mother, that's okay! If you dream of starting your own business or running a big corporation, work on that! Don't let someone else's opinion of what your life should be dictate how you should actually live your life. Whatever makes you happy, do that! Make a conscious effort to be satisfied. And when you aren't, do something about it. That is a part of your responsibility to yourself. Put that effort in. You deserve it!

Love yourself and put yourself first. ALWAYS. Show others just how you should be loved by how you love yourself. Don that oxygen mask. Fill your cup ALL the way up. Whatever metaphor you want to use, just practice self-care. Don't wait around for someone else to take care of you and pamper you and love you. Do it your damn self. It will mean more coming from you. Focus on yourself more than anyone else in your life. Spend your time doing what makes you happy and doing what is best for you. Take care of your mind, soul, and body! Your physical, emotional, mental, and spiritual happiness and well-being are your obligations to yourself.

Don't live for other people. Don't worry about what others think, and don't even try to impress others. Do things that impress yourself, and the right people will surround you. Find things that make you happy. It's very possible to care about everyone—and I mean everyone—without giving a fuck about what they think. It's pretty simple to me.

And lastly, don't worry about how many others have quit on you. Just NEVER quit on yourself. Keep pushing yourself until you get to where you want to be. You might get low at times, but as long as you keep putting that effort into yourself, you haven't given up. Sometimes you may need a pause—take a nap and wake up rejuvenated to push yourself after you have gotten to a place where you can. Fall down, but get right back up. You owe it to yourself.

OTHERS matter too, so surround yourself with good people:

Surround yourself with people who are rooting for you. Always. The people who are on your team. Those who love you in the rain and sun. Those who love you through your beauty and your blemishes. Those who love you at your highest and your lowest. Those who cheer for you, support you, and see the awesome inside of you. These are the people to always have in your life. Everyone else can kick rocks.

Everyone deserves a chance at happiness. Don't feed into the political bullshit. Breastfeed in public, fight for gay rights, accept interracial dating, let transgender individuals have their bathrooms, who cares! There are people who don't have bathrooms, food, or a place to lay their heads. The things we fight about are sometimes first-world problems. Let others do what makes them happy, mind your own business, and do what makes you happy. Regardless of where we are in our lives, can we just agree that everyone deserves a chance at happiness? So what if someone is different than me? I am going to love and respect them anyway. In fact, my husband is a Republican, and I am not loyal to any political party. Whichever candidate makes the most promises of LOVE is the candidate I vote for. If I can love my husband anyway, you can love those different than you, too.

This one is very important—love someone who treats you better than you treat yourself. Be kind to yourself, but make sure your partner is even kinder to you. This will matter on those days that you want to give up. Your better half will step in and pull your share and theirs until you can take back over. Don't feel bad about it. One day, you will be the one pulling the entire load. It all balances out in the end.

Always make time for the people you choose to have in your life. If you keep your circle small with just the right people in it, you will find time for them all. You may not always be able to drop what you are doing and run when you are needed, but those who love you will understand the efforts you are able to put in. When they pop in your head, reach out to them. Tell them you are thinking about them. Be special to them. And honestly, a positive way to assure your own success is to build up those in your circle. Once you have determined who is worthy to be in your life, promote them! Lift them up! Support their businesses and tell others about them.

Respect people, always. All people. Lift everyone you encounter up, even those you won't allow in your circle. Love the people who treat you right and pray for the ones who don't. It's okay to be selective with who you confide in. I call it being selectively social. Don't try to work out relationships that are not meant for you. The fewer people you chill with, the less bullshit you deal with.

And finally, be okay with letting go of unhealthy relationships. Not everyone was meant to be in your life for the entire journey. It really is better to be alone than to be with someone who doesn't have your best interests at heart or someone who brings you unhappiness. Therefore, surround yourself with people who make you a better person. If there is a person in your life weighing you down, the best thing you can do for yourself AND for them is to let them go. You can love them from afar, but if you continue to allow them in your life, it will turn into a downward spiral, affecting every relationship you try to have.

. . .

<u>**USE words wisely:**</u>

Learn to control your tongue. I know this sounds funny coming from someone whose favorite word is "fuck"! But for real...words are very powerful. Use them to build people up, not tear them down. You can't take back harsh words, so think prior to reacting. It will save a lot of relationships.

I have learned that silence can never be misunderstood. Don't waste words on people who deserve your silence. Use this powerful tool when you need to—it just might save you.

And most importantly, speak only "good" to yourself. What you tell yourself every day will either tear you down or lift you up. Whatever you tell yourself, that's what will come to be. So be kind to everyone but especially to yourself.

<u>**BE intentional:**</u>

Intentionally laugh until you can't laugh anymore. It is your responsibility to do things that make you laugh. And as they say, laughter is the best medicine! Proverbs 17:22 says, "A cheerful heart is good medicine," so it has always been known. I have literally gotten this far in life with laughter. It is so good for the soul. We aren't designed to be miserable. We were made to be happy and cheerful.

So watch comedy movies. Hang around your funny friends. Look up funny memes. Just think about a time when something hilarious happened to you. Search YouTube for funniest home videos, funniest animals, or whatever your heart wants to see at that moment. If you can't think of anything, start a joke jar! Every time you hear a funny joke, write it down and put it in a jar to pick from later whenever you are in need of a good laugh. Do this often.

Don't stress. There is always tomorrow. You have survived

every one of your bad days and everything nasty you have had to endure in this life. And here you are! You're killing it! Some days you will need rest. Take all the time you need, but clear your mind and de-stress purposefully.

Follow the list you created in Chapter 4 of things that bring you happiness. Do at least one thing from this list. Every. Single. Day. Intentionally.

Find a good church family. It is so important to surround yourself with people who hold the same beliefs as you. Learn from them; join them in being Jesus' hands and feet. I say this as I sit here not having attended church regularly in years. I occasionally attend my pastor's church. I haven't really gotten to know anyone else in that church, and finding a good home church is on my to-do list.

Find a career that makes you happy, something you are passionate about. You spend more of your awake time at work than you do anywhere else, so it is imperative that you find employment that you enjoy. I sell real estate and work from home, among other means of making a living and multiple streams of income. It works perfectly for our family, and I have always been all over the place, so it works great for me.

If you find yourself in a job that isn't a good fit for you and it is sucking the life out of you, you owe it to yourself to seek something different. When I was young, it was very common for people to find a job and stick to it for their entire life. They were called "lifers." And then, they'd collect a pension from their jobs when they retired. That isn't common anymore, and we find that when retirement comes, a lot of us are left to fend for ourselves. If that was the reason most people stayed at their job, and that is rarely available anymore, then why not pack up and start over? I am not suggesting you up and quit without having a plan. But work on that plan and then take action! Begin correcting your resume and sending it out. Apply for jobs that tug at your heart. Those are the most meaningful. When you find something, be respectful and put in a notice. You always want to have a good reference if anything should happen.

Recently, I discovered that it isn't really real estate that I am in love with—it is the act of helping people who are struggling or have been dealt a bad hand find stability with homeownership. I have spent a lot of my life helping people get their credit right and think about employment and debt-to-income ratios in order to get to a place where they can make a difference and get on their feet. This is my passion. Find your passion, and don't quit until you get it.

Be intentional in building a life from which you will never need a vacation. One where you can live every day happy and relaxed as if every day was a vacation, at home and at work. In all ways, live a life you enjoy.

Be purposely impactful. Someone is waiting on you to impact them. What can you do today to make a difference in someone's life?

Stay on your mission. Sometimes, it may feel like you have a lot on your plate, but like Saratoga Lynx says, "I can't cry about having a lot on my plate when my goal was to eat!" Sometimes, being busy is good! Fill that plate up and follow the plan you have set for your life! Saratoga Lynx also said, "Chew with your mouth open for the people who hate to see you eating," and "Don't let your food get cold worrying about what's on my plate." Yes, I like food, and I like food quotes, but she relates to me in some kinda way. I am a go-getter. My plate is always full. And I couldn't care less what others think or what they got going on on their plate. Unless they need help eating it. Then I am there to assist.

At the same time, pick your battles in life. I once went to a birthday party for a friend's child, and an older woman was sitting by me. My young son, who wasn't far into potty training, had to pee and wanted to do so outside. She was very rude, telling me that she couldn't believe I would allow this and that that was why there were toilets, etc. Needless to say, he whipped it out at that party that day, concealed, of course, and we enjoyed the rest of the party. No one ever saw it, and I didn't have to explain myself to her. Just let your kid pee outside! Geez!

Be authentic to yourself and to others. Be real. Be raw. Be genuine. Be purposeful in giving out positive light, positive energy, and positive vibes authentically. And always keep growing as a person. You are in complete control of how you see your life. If you learn new information and find you were wrong with previous beliefs, it is okay to change your mind. Own yourself. That is authenticity. Keep wondering and learning and growing. Keep striving to become who you are, the real authentic you.

Always pursue understanding. If you get in a rut and don't understand life, talk to a child. Sometimes, it takes the innocence of a child to understand life again! Or maybe you need the wisdom of an elder. Always pursue the knowledge of new people. Network. Get out there and meet people! Goodness is all around us. We just have to find it!

Realize that no one has to understand your life. It isn't for them to try to comprehend. Get your life together. Working on yourself is one of the hardest parts of life. My soul feels deeply, but I have learned that the fewer fucks I give, the better my life gets. This isn't to say that I have no sympathy—I just love myself THAT much! I am tough, thick-hearted, and don't take offense easily—mainly because other people's opinions of me don't determine who I am. My only concern is how I feel about myself.

And it took me a long time to understand that. I'm intentional in how I think of myself. You should be, too.

Intentionally invest in life—in your own life and the life of others. I like to focus on those in need. Specifically, those in transition and in need. A veteran transitioning into civilian life. A foster child aging out of the system. A recently divorced, now single mom. I feel this is my calling. And since one of my recent words of the year for myself is "ALIGNMENT," I focus on purposely placing people and events in line with my vision for myself. I align my health goals, love goals, financial, and business goals, my goals for happiness, and my spiritual goals together for the common purpose of fulfillment. Intentionally.

LIVE in the NOW:

I have realized and accepted that there will always be complications, and therefore I put my effort into being happy in the "right now." So, do something from your list today. Right now!

Don't wait for anything. Don't wait for the perfect job, or the perfect moment, or the perfect house, or the perfect friend. Life goes faster than you think, and perfection is a myth. Live your life to the fullest each and every day, and when you get to the end of your life, you will feel no regrets. You will look back and see that, even though the steps along the way weren't perfect, the life you have lived happened just the way it needed to. And it was perfect.

Live in the present! Always. Be here physically and mentally. Right here, right where you are. Just BE.

Don't live in the past. You are no longer there, and you can't change anything about it, so forgive yourself and move on.

Don't live in the future. It hasn't come yet. And if you keep trying to live somewhere that isn't here yet, it may never come, and you will miss out on some very important things in the here and now.

In all facets of life, always make the conscious choice to be content NOW. Don't wait until life is easier, or better, or less busy. Don't wait until you have more time, more money, or more joy. Create your own joy. There is never such a thing as "ready," so don't ever say, "I will when I am ready." "Ready" will never come. Don't spend your life saving money, hoping that you can buy your happiness later because later may never come. Find it now before you run out of time. Live life right now before it is over. In a blink of an eye, you will go from 16 to 60. Don't let it pass you by. LIVE. NOW!

EXONERATE yourself:

Use your life experiences as motivation. Find peace, even in the chaos. Don't be embarrassed of your past. God will use your story to restore others. Let Him! I definitely have a colorful past, and sometimes it was dark. I've made good and bad choices, I've taken risks, I've accomplished some amazing feats, and I've fallen very low in my short life. And through it all, I continue to learn and do better than the day before. I have freed myself from the bondage of captivity within my own mind. You can, too! Just let go of anything that is weighing you down. Get rid of all negativity and only focus on positive thoughts. Let go and just be. Pardon yourself from the bad and look forward to the good.

SERVE:

And what better way to make up for some bad decisions than to serve others? Work hard on being a good person. Focus on not only doing good things for yourself, but also doing good things for other people and for this world that we live in. Review Chapter 7 for a list of ways to pay it forward.

Smile at everyone. If you have the power to make someone happy, do it. Anyone can find dirt on someone...be the one to find gold. Making people feel good is definitely having a serving spirit.

Plant a seed. Sow seeds of love. Those receiving may not be ready for change now, but be the seed. And sometimes, you ARE literally the seed. Sometimes, you are in a dark place and feel buried alive, but you later find that it was then that you were planted. So even in hard times, the way you are responding is planting seeds for others. Start now, and you have the ability to change an entire future generation.

START (slowly if you must), but don't be afraid to START OVER again and again:

Take baby steps. If you can't do what is best for you right now, do what's best for your children or your spouse or whoever. Start there. And eventually, you will begin to realize that you are worthy. You are needed on this earth. And you will begin to see your value.

If you feel like you have hit rock bottom, let rock bottom become the solid foundation to rebuild your life upon. Heal and restore to become even greater than you were before. Rock bottom can build you into the awesome diva that you are!

Realize every day is a new day to start over. If the day didn't go as you planned, rest, then get back up and kick ass. Wake up every morning with a grateful heart. You aren't under any obligation to be the person you were even a minute ago, so if you learn something and feel like changing your mind, then do it! If you were wrong in your mind or heart yesterday, fix it today! Even the worst days have only 24 hours. Let every day be a new beginning, a fresh start, and a chance to be happy. Take advantage of the sunset and sunrise. They demonstrate daily renewal.

And when you get to a painful ending, you may realize it is just the new beginning. Life is the way you make it. The choices you make. The actions you take. Make your own happy ending. Play some gangsta rap music or whatever your soul needs in that moment and just LIVE, starting over again and again if necessary.

I never worry about whether my glass is half empty or half full. You know why? Because my glass will always be refillable.

It might take some hard work to not be miserable, but I have total faith that once you get into the groove, you will have a blast finding savage self-contentment! Being happy is so good for your wellness! Christian author J. Stanford said, "Health is a state of body. Wellness is a state of being." Start being!

Inside of my Skin
Inside of my skin,
I am within myself,
From the day I am born til the day I decease,
From the time I awake til the time that I slept.
I put all of my effort into finding myself.
And loving me. Outside and in.

I can't escape,
My thoughts engulf me.
I hear them all day and all night,
So I make sure I speak love and light.
I talk good to myself.

I take care of my body.

It is here that I dwell.
Here I will always reside in my sanctuary.
I must treat it well. From the way that I dress
To the way that I smell.
Not for those around, but for me.
My tattoos tell my story.
I am a canvas.

I can't take a break from myself for even a moment,
But that's okay.
Because I've realized that I am the shit,
So I love myself and care for myself,
Even if I am the only one to obey
The boundaries that I've set for me.

Happiness comes from within alone.
It's nobody else's burden to bear.
I am worthy, I am loved,
I am well, I am being.
I am responsible for my inner-peace.
Inside of my skin.
I find enjoyment in me.

Maintaining your happiness is your responsibility. Make a daily promise to yourself to do whatever it takes to make life good.

It doesn't really matter the reason why I started working on a good life—all that matters is that I did it, and BOY, IS IT GOOD!

At the end of the first chapter of the Bible, Genesis, it describes the beginning, the creation of heaven and earth, and all of the good stuff about how we came into being. God looked at all that He had made, which was amazing, by the way! And He gave Himself a pat on the back. He said, "it was good."

Go on now and get out there to work on not just making your life good, but purposefully maintaining this good life. And not just any good life—a SAVAGE good life!

You got this! I'm rooting for you!

Self-Reflection:

1. Do you have a list of ways that you maintain your happiness that aren't on this list? I would love to hear them! Please send them to me at commahappyenjoythepause@gmail.com.

____

____

____

____

____

____

2. Read above on ways to LAUGH. Start that joke jar. You can put in it things that have happened that have made you laugh so you can reminisce or write down funny jokes as you hear them. Anything worthy of a good laugh, give energy to it, put it in writing, and stick it in the jar (and as always, if you have a funny joke, please send it to me at commahappyenjoythepause@gmail.com so I can add it to my joke jar).

____

____

____

____

____

3. Create a mantra for yourself. I alternate between two a lot—"I am a warrior" and "I am savage." I am fierce, and I fight for myself. I don't let anyone else do this for me. Maybe I should just say, "I am a savage warrior," ha! Every day when you wake up, chant your mantra to remind yourself what a badass you are and to kick-start your day in the right direction.

____

____

____

____

____

chapter 146

THOU SHALT STRIVE FOR SELF-TRANSCENDENCE

According to Maslow's hierarchy of needs, we must build our foundation (or the base of the pyramid) by meeting the most basic of needs. This comes in the form of the air we breathe, food, water, sleep, and shelter. We cannot reach our full potential if we cannot meet our basic needs. So this must happen first and foremost.

From here, we go a step higher and focus on the need to feel connection and safety. This can be having a secure home, secure job, the absence of violence, and the freedom to be creative.

Next, we can begin to focus on love and meaningful relationships. And from there, we go to the regard others have for us as well as the esteem we feel for ourselves. This includes speaking our own truth and feeling self-certainty.

At the top of this pyramid lies self-actualization. Total fulfillment. Reaching your full potential. Meeting the goals you have set for yourself.

We can't stop there, however! Once our basic needs are met and we work our way up this pyramid, we must always strive for constant betterment. The continuous need to keep ascending up this pyramid is the driving force to our final height of human development. At this point, we connect with the universe and meet our maker head-on by reaching down and bringing people up to this level with us. We realize that being the HANDS AND FEET is an energy only found in the supernatural with the understanding of universal unity. Once we realize that our family, or our community, or even strangers for that matter, are taken care of by those passing by them and through their life in that moment in time, we finally understand that we are united by the bond of helping each other and lifting each other up.

It's that simple! What fulfillment would we get by getting to the top and looking down on others?

NONE!

So later in Maslow's life, he added on to and expanded his hierarchy of needs as he understood it. Most importantly, he added that once you realize self-actualization, you must then help the next person reach their self-actualization. He called this self-transcendency. This means helping others meet their needs altruistically. Maintaining happiness is so important, and we can find that primarily by blessing others.

I also made a connection with the chakra system. The root chakra focuses on our foundation—our basic needs of survival and feeling secure. As we work our way up, we put our energy into ourselves: our emotions, our power, and our self-esteem. We go on to put effort into love for self and for others and express ourselves and have our voices heard. We go up this ladder and make it to our intuition, our wisdom, and finally to self-real-ization.

This energy system can be altered by the foods we eat, the way we think, and the things we do. Sometimes, these changes are subtle, and sometimes they're LOUD. But all the steps we take are important. My ultimate goal is to realize myself so that I can be at a place where I can reach down and help others around me be fulfilled.

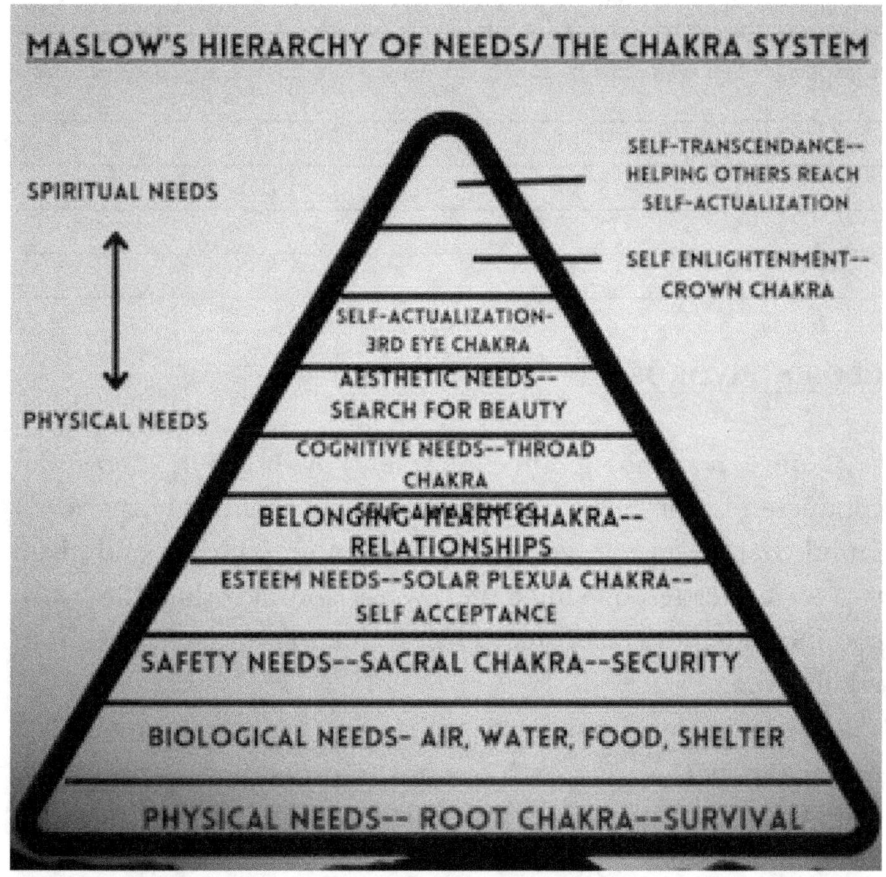

Self-Reflection:

1. What's holding you down? Have you made it to self-actualization? Have you found fulfillment in yourself? If not, what is stopping you? Once you get there, you are unstoppable

and you can begin the cycle to help the next person! The world is in your hands at this point. Self-transcendence is SAVAGE!

____

____

____

____

____

____

CLOSING WORDS:

I once read about an experiment by Bruce K. Alexander conducted in the 1970s. Prior to this experiment, it was already found that when rats were placed in an empty cage and given two water bottles, one filled with water and the other filled with cocaine water, the rats consistently drank the cocaine water until it killed them.

But in Bruce Alexander's experiment, he placed rats in "rat parks" where they had both options to drink, but they also had everything they could ever imagine: places to rest, have sex, eat food, and everything good. And in this study, the rats did not drink the cocaine water to their deaths. They only drank it until they felt good. Then, they quit.

This tells me that the fix for addiction is to change your environment. Surround yourself with good things and good people. Change your habits. Get to know yourself and gravitate towards things that make you happy. When you need to take a pause, do so. Tomorrow is a new day to kick ass and do kick-ass things that you enjoy doing.

There was another study done by Dr. Curt Richter who

placed rats in water to test how long they can stay above. On average, they would give up and begin to sink after 15 minutes. Before they would completely give up from exhaustion, he would grab them and dry them off, then give them a place to rest for a few. Then, he would put them back in again. Only this time, they would last on average 60 HOURS. Do you know what this means? With a little rest and some faith in humanity, there is so much hope for not just surviving through life, but enjoying a fan-fuck-ing-tastic life at that.

A pause can do everyone some good. We are all rats in this rat race called life. What matters most is how we live, how we love, and how we serve.

I've lived my life as a fatherless child. I let it define me when I should have used it for fuel to change the future for other chil-dren who felt alone and abandoned. This was a part of my align-ment, and once I figured this out, I really started living.

I've used the word alignment throughout this book. This word has been the basis for me in writing this book. I am working on being intentional to do my part in not just my own alignment, but the alignment of others around me. There is never a final destination until death. And even then, who knows? No one has ever survived death. For all I know, death is just a passageway to something even grander! Until then, we are simply jumping from pause to pause...stone to stone.

<u>Alignment</u>
A wild ride through the cosmos,
An awakening from my genesis
Every second in time...every breath...every step,
From the top of the world to every moment of death I've kissed.
Everything I've endured has led me to this.
Order in the madness, when it doesn't make sense,

Systematically arranged, organized in such a way
That at the end of each phase—I gasp,
Excited for what's to come next.

My moments are measured by fractions of chance,
People coming and going, regulated by the stars.
I weep, and it feels like I suffer alone,
Wither and wilting into the abyss
Until an atomic moment in time, I arise from the void a warrior.

The universe orients and conforms as if revolving around me.
Divine intervention that the sun rises and sets
at just the right time,
And each time a series of events had to happen,
A woven, complicated web, a coincidental destiny.
Sometimes intentional but often by chance
Either way, a predestined circumstance.

This life of fate, true karma at work.
The life behind me, the world to come.
Each moment leading to the next outcome,
And the next and the next, until that final fate,
Which leads me to the next thing I can't escape.
The past is my future, the future my past.
If you don't look close, it may seem like chance,
Each detail separate, not a big deal
When aligned together, sizably vast.
Whether by fate or by design, my life has been aligned,
Demonstrating the impossible is imaginable!
My alignment was paved specifically for me.

Every heartbeat of my life, I am living a movement,

My vision is coming to fruition by the powers that be
Who are always looking out for me.
My alignment has always been intentional, even if not by me.
By the Universe, the Supreme Being, Divinity,
The Spirits found in you and in me.
All aligning for the better good of humanity.

It may not seem like it in the moment
When tragedy and chaos erupt, your world in shambles,
It is then that divinity is preparing you for battle.
Goodness is coming, the stars are aligning,
And in just the right timing, birth is given to this version of you,
Perfectly designed to face what's to come.
Your alignment brings you to where you are needed.
The universe is preparing you—
Free yourself, and get ready for your alignment.
It happens in an instant, and then,
you are back to waiting and preparing,
Being a part of someone else's alignment
Until the next moment the Universe has you in Her grasp.

I am a nomad, a free spirit, always wandering to find my next moment in time, my next happy stone. I'll never forget where I came from, but I have found abundant blessings in knowing and trusting myself to always seek savage happiness. Sometimes I plan ahead, but a lot of times, I design my road map as I go. I know that life is about each step we take and each person we come in contact with. And step by step, stone by stone, we meander through life with the power inside of us to alter our existence. When bad is thrown at me, I fortify from within and change course, even before I get to that next stepping stone.

The African concept of "ubuntu" has been such a part of my

life; it means "I am because we are." In this way of life, I am who I am through other people. My humanity is fostered by my relations with others. I pick up things from others and take them as my own. A part of them becomes a part of me. Our commonality means so much more than any of us as individuals or any divisions that may exist between us. There is a universal bond, and we are all connected. I serve, then they serve. One day, someone serves me, and I continue the circle. We are one. We achieve ourselves by sharing a part of ourselves with those around us. We live on by passing on our goodness to others. That is our legacy, and each of us is legendary!

We walk alone, we walk with others. Others share their journeys, then disperse to their own journey alone. A constant web of intertwining between and within each other.

UBUNTU.

I am because we are. The steps I take are because of the relationships I have formed. The direction I go next will be guided by the next person I encounter. And my life goal will be to build myself up with the spirit of reaching down to help the next person up.

Who will you meet, and what path will your stepping stones lead you on next on this circular journey of multidimensional elevated human connection and fulfillment?

epilogue

A while ago, I ran across a verse, John 14: 2, that says, "In my Father's house are many rooms," and I felt a tug to set on a journey to find a home with many rooms or land with many homes so I can prepare a place for those in need. I'm still working on finding a large parcel of land to fulfill this need…but until then, we have a few extra rooms in the new house that we just built and moved into, and we will continue to help the children displaced in the foster care system. The new home will give us enough space to keep large sibling groups together. That has always been a wish of mine. And the doors of our new home are finally open, and I am embarking on the journey of crossing paths with those I was always meant to cross paths with.

I also recently sold my CBD store and used the proceeds to purchase three lots only one mile away from my new house where I can grow my new business. I am growing a space where we can have a community. My goal for the new business is to focus on overall well-being. We all have some facet in life in which we are not quite fulfilled. So I wanted to focus on a space where we can find our BEST life and feel the most ALIVE we can feel. A place where we can focus on not just self-care, but also care for others. Finding balance within ourselves so we can then help others find it too. After all, we are all connected. Whether we are aware of it or not, our happiness is dependent on one another. I will begin this venture online and grow it into an amazing addition to our new neighborhood. Please, follow us at http://www.commahappyhealthclub.com as we make progress.

It's now 2022, and my word of the year is "SIMPLIFY"! I think I started it off well and am knocking off so many items on my checklist. What relief I feel with each check mark...and I know it sounds crazy to think I am simplifying with all of this change going on, but just wait until I follow through with everything on my checklist. A weight is being lifted already!

I have been struggling within a bit. I guess you can say I'm soul-searching again. I have a hard time with some of the wrath that comes from a depicted loving God and the cult-like demeanor of the church. I resonate with a little bit of this religion and a little bit of that. And I'm studying, spending a lot of time being still, and letting my divine insight guide me. I am still a spiritual being and recognize when I'm feeling off-balance, so I'm addressing it.

And finally, the biggest news of all...Tanner, you know, the one to whom this book is dedicated...my 17-year-old, firstborn, the first love of my life?

Yeah—him...

He is going to be a daddy. I am finally past shock and have melted into AWWWWW...

Yes, he is young. But he has been with his girlfriend for well over a year. He loves her. He has a reliable truck. He has a good job working for a contractor. He has finished school this year with a certificate in carpentry and will hopefully go on to obtain his contractor's license. He knows his place as the father of the baby, and he is taking responsibility. He has vowed to never be like his father and to make sure his baby can always count on him.

I admit that I don't know how to parent my child who is going to be a parent. This is all new to me. And being the mother of the daddy is hard because his girlfriend handles her business, and Tanner is just like, *"Whatever she says is what's going to be for this baby."* And I can't even be mad at him because I am a mom, and I always knew no man was ever going to tell me what is best for my children.

HA!

He just had his gender reveal party–and he is having a BOY! Yikes! And my pastor friend came and spoke love over them. It was perfect.

I added him to my credit card a few months ago to start building his credit, and he just closed on his very first house for his sweet little family. It's a fixer-upper, but he can handle it, and it is only four miles from me, so I can just hop in my car and spoil my grandbaby any time I want to.

I was nervous for him at first, but as I spoke with a friend of mine who heartbreakingly just lost her newborn, she said, "Let the babies have babies!" She feels like she waited too long, but Tanner—he has a chance to do so many good things and create the perfect little family.

A family he will always be responsible for and never walk away from.

I couldn't be any more proud than I am at this moment.

He is ending the curse of babies being raised without a father. He is taking the steps and changing the path that will affect all of his children and his children's children.

UBUNTU.

Life is about taking steps and forming relationships that are guided by a higher being, intentionally building ourselves up to a point where we can then reach down and help those around us. That's literally the meaning of a well-lived life. For me, anyway!

And that's a wrap! Call it a day. That's all she wrote...for now. Till next time! As Jim Carey says, "I have an insane belief in my own ability to manifest things. I believe we're creators, and I believe we create with every thought and every word. Every moment is PREGNANT with the next moment of your life."

It's that simple...UBUNTU. Align. Simplify. Manifest the moments of your life. Let every moment be pregnant with the next moment. And give birth to a comma happy, savage good life.

Jennifer Rose Elliott is authentic and raw, messy and fervent. A poet at heart, she speaks to the wild and untamed as well as those more polished who occasionally trip up. After all, everyone is human. My, what a life she has lived: She's a mom, a foster mother, a surrogate mother, a military spouse, a veteran of the US Army NG, and a graduate from Liberty University with a BS in business management.

An entrepreneur, an employee at times, a business owner, and a real estate broker—many different walks in life make up the fascinating life of Jennifer Rose Elliott. And her greatest achievement? Finding self-contentment in the chaos of this crazy thing we call life in order to achieve comma happy, SAVAGE happiness.